The Retreat Leaders' Guide

GRACE NOTES

The Retreat Leaders' Guide

J. Michael Sparough, SJ

Diane Michutka Fraser • Mary Anne Reese

Charis
MINISTRIES

Ignatian Spirituality for Men and Women in Their 20s and 30s

Excerpts from the *New American Bible* with Revised New Testament and Psalms. Copyright © 1991, 1986, 1970 Confraternity of Christian Doctrine, Inc., Washington, DC. All rights reserved. No portion of the *New American Bible* may be reprinted without permission in writing from the copyright holder.

Cover design by Kathryn Seckman Kirsch
Interior design by Maggie Hong

Every effort has been made to locate the copyright holders for the cited works used in this publication and to make full acknowledgment for their use. In the case of any omissions, the Publisher will be pleased to make suitable acknowledgments in future editions.

ISBN-13: 978-0-8294-2521-5
ISBN-10: 0-8294-2521-7

Printed in the United States
08 09 10 11 12 13 TPS 10 9 8 7 6 5 4 3 2 1

Contents

Welcome to Charis Retreats 1

Program Overview 4

1 Goals and Assumptions of a Charis Retreat 7

2 Before You Begin: Preparing for Success 20

3 Designing the Model: Movements of a Charis Retreat 36

4 Selecting and Preparing the Team 51

5 Sharing the Story: Developing and Giving Retreat Talks . . . 65

6 Starting the Retreat: Christian Hospitality and Welcome . . . 73

7 Creating and Tending Small Groups 82

8 Offering Spiritual Resources 93

9 After the Retreat: Journeys Ended, Journeys Begun 105

10 Adaptations of Charis Programs 115

Conclusion 125

Acknowledgments 127

Endnotes 129

Index 131

Welcome to Charis Retreats

Welcome, and thank you for dedicating yourself to the important work of nurturing the spiritual needs of adults in their twenties and thirties.

Allow us to begin by telling you something you already know: Young adults are drifting away from Catholic and mainline Protestant churches, finding them increasingly irrelevant to their spiritual quest.

Now let us tell you something you might not know: A retreat of spiritual renewal can plant seeds of change in young adults that will have a profound and lasting spiritual impact.

Young adults can be difficult to reach through mainstream church channels. Yet Charis retreats have had life-changing effects for more than a thousand young adults who have made these retreats and days of prayer. Many of these retreatants were eventually trained as team members.

Rooted in Ignatian Spirituality

Charis Ministries was founded in Chicago in 2000 to continue the 450-year tradition of innovation in spirituality begun by St. Ignatius of Loyola.

Ignatius grew up in the golden age of sixteenth-century Spain. Until age thirty, he lived a privileged life of self-indulgence as a Spanish military officer. Then one day, while engaged in a perilous battle, he was badly wounded when a cannonball struck his leg. While recovering from this life-threatening injury, he began reading about the lives of the saints and experienced a deep spiritual conversion. The conversion was so profound that he decided to leave behind his life of privilege and to spend the rest of his days teaching others how to experience God's love and how to make important life decisions.

Ignatius taught that just as the body needs exercise, so does the soul. Because of his Spiritual Exercises, which have stood the test of time as a significant means of spiritual conversion, Ignatius was named the patron saint of retreats. He founded the Society of Jesus, or the Jesuits, and taught all his followers to engage the world by becoming "contemplatives in action." Ignatius believed that taking the time to reflect on one's life experience was the surest path to God's grace. This notion is the mission of Charis retreats for young adults today.

At the heart of our mission are life-changing spiritual exercises designed specifically for the needs of today's young adults in their twenties and thirties, both married and single. These exercises are designed to be largely peer-led and to draw on the personal experience of the team and of the retreatants as pathways to the sacred.

Building on Success

Charis retreats build on the insights of many retreat and renewal programs that have proved successful since the Second Vatican Council, such as Cursillo, Marriage Encounter, Christ Renews His Parish, Teens Encounter Christ (TEC), KAIROS teen retreats, and others. All employ at least four basic building blocks: peer witness, structured silent reflection, facilitated small-group sharing, and innovative ritual and liturgy. These are the legs on which most contemporary retreat programs have been built, and Charis shares much of the same approach.

Charis retreats are different from those mentioned, however, in at least three significant ways. First, Charis weekends and days of prayer are among the few spiritual renewal programs targeted specifically toward adults

> **Charis** (kâr′ĭs) n. 1. From the Greek word meaning "grace", "mercy", or "God moments." 2. Ignatian Spirituality for Young Adults (from St. Ignatius of Loyola). v. 3. To take young adults in their twenties and thirties to inspired places. 4. To recognize we are in the heart of God.

in their twenties and thirties. The generation gap is significant; ignoring the differences of age and culture places contemporary evangelization in great peril.

Second, many retreat and renewal programs are one-time events or entry-level programs of initiation designed to inaugurate a spiritual rebirth. Once the retreatants have participated in this program, they have had "the experience." What remains is to share the experience with others. Charis certainly does this, as the most effective team members are often those who have been deeply touched by making the retreat themselves. But Charis is also deeply committed to the ongoing development of other programs of spiritual renewal that address a wide variety of topics vital to young adult seekers. Think of Charis as infinite variations on themes of importance to young adults. To date, Charis has developed the retreat models listed in the box to the right.

Finally, Charis retreats incorporate elements of our faith tradition, such as catechesis and religious education, for a generation whose catechesis is often lacking. Some retreat programs do this. Many do not, opting simply for a personal-experience model. Charis retreats initiate a dialogue that involves our personal experience, our faith tradition, and our culture. We have seen lives change dramatically and subtly through the impact of these retreats. It is our hope that they will be of significant service to young adults everywhere. &

Retreat Models

- The Seekers' Retreat: The Search for Faith
- Who Do You Say I Am? The Jesus Retreat
- Called and Chosen: Renewing Our Catholic Commitment
- The Spirit at Work Within: Discerning Our Gifts
- Sex in the City of God: Faith, Intimacy, and Relationships
- Peace and Justice: Catholic Social Teaching
- Decisions! Decisions! and Transitions That Follow

Program Overview

Grace Notes: Charis Young Adult Retreats is a series that consists of two main components. The first component is *The Retreat Leaders' Guide*, which you are reading. It offers the theological and pastoral foundation for the retreats and describes the practical steps necessary to implement the program. These steps include planning, promotion, team selection and training, logistics, evaluation, and follow-up. This introductory volume provides an overview of all the Charis retreats.

Charis Retreat Guide

The volume you are reading, *The Retreat Leaders' Guide,* provides pastoral guidance and resource materials intended to help you launch a Charis retreat program. It is designed for young adult leaders and volunteers who want to offer a program more challenging and enriching than an evening event or a social gathering. It will be of assistance to those who organize events on the diocesan, regional, or parish level for those in their twenties and thirties. This guide will also be of help to colleges and universities that want to add depth to their retreat programs. It is for people who are working with young adults or who desire to do so. Most importantly, this guide is for the young adults themselves who are taking an active role in leadership by reaching out to their peers. Charis's hope is that the resources provided here will help your own retreat ministry prosper.

Retreat Resource Books

The retreat resource books are the other main component of *Grace Notes*. Each resource book is devoted to a specific type of Charis retreat. The resource books consist of templates, training and retreat materials, and a complete script for a weekend retreat. They also provide information for adapting the retreat to fit into one day or one overnight retreat. All the Charis retreat resources are intended to help retreatants, volunteers, and leaders make smooth transitions from one retreat experience to the next.

Now available are *The Seekers' Retreat Resource Book* and *Who Do You Say I Am? The Jesus Retreat Resource Book*. Resource books for the other Charis retreats may be available at a later date.

Web Resources

Charis retreat materials are available on the Internet. Visit www .CharisRetreats.org to download electronic templates for schedules, publicity materials, example retreat talks, and more. Many of these materials can be customized on your computer. ⚛

> Visit **www.CharisRetreats.org** to download retreat materials and customize them on your computer.

CHAPTER 1

Goals and Assumptions
of a Charis Retreat

Charis retreats are designed to meet the specific needs of people between twenty and forty years of age—to help them recognize God's presence in every aspect of their lives. This group of young adults, often referred to as Generation X and Millennials (also known as Generation Y), has common identifiable needs and concerns. To best minister to these young adults, we have explored these needs, as well as developmental, emotional, cultural, and spiritual issues often encountered by Catholics born after the Second Vatican Council.

This guide is designed to support you in leading a Charis retreat. Through practical suggestions, background information, and sample talks, the guide will help you create an environment that allows retreatants to best examine their relationship with God.

In the following sections, we will discuss some of the identifiable needs of young adults and introduce the theological, pastoral, and cultural foundations of our retreats.

The Needs of Young Adults

Young adults, especially those in their twenties and early thirties, often struggle to define themselves. They confront a variety of questions during this time of self-discovery. The U.S. Catholic Bishops' *Sons and Daughters of the Light: A Pastoral Plan for Ministry with Young Adults*[1] notes the following issues that young adults face, each of which Charis retreats are intended to help its participants address.

Developing Personal Identity

We often hear identity-related questions from young adults such as these: Who am I? How do I deal with the hurts of childhood, adolescence, or present life? If this is the best time of my life, why am I depressed or lonely?

Developing Relationships

In regard to relationships, young adults often pose the following questions: Who will be my life partner? Do I want a life partner (yet)? How can I be intimate with others emotionally and physically without fear? What role does my family of origin play in my life, and do I want that role to change? How do I integrate my sexual feelings in a healthy and positive way?

Developing a Definition of Work

We frequently hear the following career-related questions: What will I do for work? Will my work be meaningful? Will my current occupation be my career, or can I "get a job" and decide what I want to do with my life later?

The Charis Approach

We believe young adults are best able to confront and work out the developmental and emotional concerns that underlie those questions when they do so in relationship with others. Charis retreats take seriously these concerns and the struggle to address them. We can provide a place and a community of peers with whom to discuss and begin to work out these concerns.

Cultural Awareness

For the generations born after 1965, the cultural setting in which they were raised was radically different from that of their parents and grandparents. Sociologists such as George Barna,[2] as well as young adult authors,[3] describe how different the generations are from their predecessors, particularly in terms of religious practice, exposure to media, and experience of broken relationships.

Men and women in their twenties and thirties have been exposed to a variety of media throughout their lives—print, radio, TV, Internet, movies, and more. Since childhood, marketers have targeted them to consume everything from soft drinks to clothing to video games to movies. Consumerism, the desire to possess everything from the latest technology to education to experiences, has had a profound impact on the development of young adults. They have been inundated with daily advances in technology and flooded with images of sex without commitment. They have lived by their watches with daily routines of daycare, classes, after-school activities, TV programs, and parents' work schedules. These young adults have felt this time crunch their entire lives and have picked up the culture's desire for achievement. In short, as theology professor Tom Beaudoin has said, young adults have grown up in the "amniotic fluid" of pop culture.[4]

Mass marketing and consumerism have shaped how young adults process information and respond to the world, including how they approach invitations into relationships. Young adults perceive that everyone is out to sell, buy, or cajole their vote or their loyalty for his or her own ends. As a result, trust—from peers, authorities, and especially institutions and their leaders—must be earned. When that trust is violated, the relationship is over, and the offending institution or person is ignored or attacked.

In such a culture, young adults are confronted with a struggle for meaning and intimacy. Some might suppress their feelings of meaninglessness and loneliness, choosing to cope through addictions to substances, destructive behaviors, or unhealthy relationships. Others might seek relief by living in a highly structured or hierarchical environment. Still others may have close peer groups that become their family or community. Most young adults manage to persevere on a journey, maturing and making decisions in the context of their formation, environment, and experience.[5]

Young Adult Spiritual Concerns

Charis's findings support those of recent research studies. We have noted that many young adults approach faith and their life journeys less as religious issues than as spiritual ones.[6] While religious language may be foreign to them, they are comfortable talking in terms of spirituality, and they are generally interested in what are traditionally considered religious questions and topics, such as ultimate meaning and ultimate trust.

Many in their twenties and thirties view spirituality as being separate from religion or as transcending it. They have specific spiritual hungers such as having a healthy personal identity, desiring intimacy in relationships, finding meaningful work, and possessing a life-giving spirituality.[7]

While young adults might have deep spiritual yearnings and a desire to learn about spiritualities and practices, they often lack knowledge of or integration of the Catholic faith tradition. Charis has found that young adults come with a broad but relatively shallow knowledge of more than one faith tradition. Through TV, the Internet, movies, the workplace, social experiences, and living in an increasingly diverse population, young adults might know as much about Judaism, Hinduism, Islam, New Age, and Evangelical Protestant traditions as they do about Roman Catholicism. Many possess a desire to be closer to God while struggling with damaging images of God or with how they think that God judges them.

We have found that regardless of the level of religious education, formation, or commitment to a church institution, retreatants express a real desire to learn to pray and to communicate with and be loved by the divine. They are seekers looking for answers to their many questions. They are exploring a variety of traditions and leaving no stone unturned to find resources that might assist them on their quest. As noted in Barna's study, religion itself is not shunned by young adults if faith systems provide new insights or useful perspectives to help individuals cope with life more effectively.

In short, young adults want to make contact with God, and they are starving for God's love. But unlike previous generations, the majority of today's young adults often value personal experience and feelings over church-issued doctrine.

Since the young adult population we serve is composed of two relatively distinct generations—Generation X and Millennials—we must identify some elements that distinguish the two from each other. *Gen X* generally refers to those born between 1960 and 1980. *Millennials* refers to those born between 1980 and 2000. Recent studies and articles tell us that while Gen X spent its childhood and adolescence being introduced to technologies (video games, computers, cell phones), Millennials spent theirs using, accruing, and creating new technologies. Their skills and attitudes toward technology were developed at a much earlier age than their Gen X counterparts.

While Gen Xers had the Space Shuttle explosion and MTV define their youth, Millennials dealt with the Columbine massacre and the Virginia Tech mass murder. Both lost many peers and members of their own generations when the Twin Towers were attacked on September 11, 2001. Finally, while many Gen Xers were latchkey kids who spent unsupervised hours after school, there is a perception that Millennials were more protected by adult authority figures. This suggests that Millennials are more likely to contribute to the "safe" institution than are Gen Xers, who are generally more critical and dismissive of institutions.

A recent study[8] shows that young adult Catholics of both generations have a strong Catholic identity but do not feel much of a commitment to the institutional church or its moral teaching. In general, the most committed Catholics in the study were the oldest, while the youngest groups (those born after Vatican II) were less committed. Many young adults surveyed felt that they were never taught the basic truths of the Catholic faith and assert that their religious education included a lot of process but not much content. In short, they say they do not understand their faith enough to explain it to their children.[9] While only nine percent of those surveyed were from the Millennial generation, the authors painted a dire portrait of what would happen to the Catholic Church if the trend of increasingly lower commitment levels continued with the Millennials.

On a positive note, the authors noted successively younger generations have been taught to think for themselves, to take responsibility for their relationships with God, and to differentiate between beliefs and practices they consider central to the faith and ones they consider peripheral or optional.[10] We have certainly found this to be true. Pastoral and anecdotal evidence suggest that Gen Xers, and to an even larger extent Millennials, are more interested than previous generations in helping the poor, serving those in need, protecting creation, and engaging in ecumenical and interfaith dialogue.

Sociologists have found a dominant de facto religion among teenagers in the United States, which researchers call "Moralistic Therapeutic Deism." This "religion" cuts across formal religious lines and has five basic beliefs:

1. A God exists who created and orders the world and watches over human life on earth.
2. God wants people to be good, nice, and fair to each other, according to the behavior code taught in the Bible and most world religions.
3. The central goal of life is to be happy and to feel good about oneself.
4. God does not need to be particularly involved in one's life except when God is needed to resolve a problem.
5. Good people go to heaven when they die.[11]

Charis retreat directors would be wise to be aware of this de facto religion when guiding retreatants, especially Millennials.

How Ignatian Spirituality Answers Needs

If feelings, emotions, and personal experience count more than theology and doctrine, then Ignatian spirituality can be an ideal entryway for young adults. Ignatian spirituality places an emphasis on finding God in all things, especially through living and reflecting on everyday experiences. Ignatian spirituality's incarnational nature allows young adults, who are keenly aware of their existence in the world, to access the divine in the everyday. It demonstrates that a 500-year-old spirituality is relevant today.

Young adults are at the stage of life and faith development in which their values affect decisions they make about family, jobs, graduate school, life partners, location, and more. Discernment in making large or small decisions is a stated need of young adults. Ignatian spirituality offers uncomplicated and well-developed methods of discernment.

Finally, there are several characteristically Ignatian methods of prayer that directly address young adults' cultural and spiritual needs. The *examen* is an individual prayer that makes use of the practitioner's daily experience, regardless of sex, race, class, educational level, or religious commitment. Imaginative prayer and the Spiritual Exercises of St. Ignatius of Loyola encourage the use of imagination. They work in conjunction with Gospel stories and the Catholic tradition and are helpful regardless of the person's experience or commitment to a faith tradition. A person can remain skeptical of an institution and still pray with these prayers. Young adults might even find that as these prayers bring them closer in intimacy with God, they will want to live that relationship more and more in community with others.

● ● ● ● ● ● ● ● ● ● ● ● ● ● ● ●

Throughout its retreats, Charis builds in ways for people to safely experience community and intimacy.

● ● ● ● ● ● ● ● ● ● ● ● ● ● ● ●

Applying Our Knowledge of Young Adults

In designing Charis retreats, we took into account everything noted above. We have applied the following methods to best address the needs and concerns of young adults.

Ministry of Prepared Peers

To create credibility and a level of trust that cannot be assumed if an elder team member is addressing a group of young adults, the prepared-peer approach is extremely effective in reaching young adults. All of us are drawn to events or relationships with people who are like us. Participants relate to team members through shared experiences, language, and culture. On a Charis retreat, prepared peers serve as speakers, small-group facilitators, and leaders of healing prayer.

Many team members and retreatants have come out of colleges where they had contact with campus ministries. For this reason, they often possess some experience of ministry to and with their peers.

Another reason we believe the peer approach works well is that outside of young adult ministry, the default position of the larger church is the culture of baby boomers and their elders. Those typically in authority are middle-aged or older.

The institutional church, through its priests and teachers, continues to define itself in relation to Vatican II, but today's young adults are not old enough to remember how the church operated before the council. The result is that young adults often feel marginalized on the other side of this milestone in the church, even if they do practice their Catholicism and participate in the Mass. (Many do not practice or participate at all, simply because they feel marginalized.) Therefore, it is liberating for them to be in community, on retreat, in prayer, or at worship where they can be informed, formed, and guided without harkening back to a time that most of the population, but not they, experienced. This experience allows them to develop a Catholic identity that reaches beyond being young in relation to the "real adults" in the pews. They are seen as peers with their own unique relationships to the Lord, with talents to contribute and the ability to lead the church.

> We introduce prayer and simple reflection exercises as well as Ignatian discernment methods as tools for making decisions.

Multimedia and Pop Culture

Throughout the retreat, especially at the beginning and end of each young adult leader's presentation, we use popular music, music videos, or other media. This use of various media, combined with prayer, integrates themes from popular culture that might make the talk or prayer more accessible. This builds on the Ignatian approach of finding God in all things.

Appealing to Diverse Audiences

It is unrealistic to assume that all people of a particular age range have similar life experiences and spiritualities. We believe, as Paul said in his first letter to the Corinthians, that we are members of a body, each with different gifts. Because the population of a Charis retreat is so diverse, we create a team that is itself diverse in experience and spirituality. During the development of a model and the preparation for a specific retreat, young adult team members drive the direction by suggesting ways to appeal to their diverse tastes. Their broad range of life experiences—influenced by gender, family events, education level, ethnic heritage, social class, and level of religious commitment—serves as a model and an invitation for retreatants to share their stories.[12]

Opportunities to Connect

Throughout its retreats, Charis builds in ways for people to safely experience community and intimacy. From their first telephone or e-mail inquiry, potential retreatants are welcomed. At the retreat itself, they are graciously met at the door and later introduced to the team and to one another through formal introduction or icebreakers. Peer team members present their stories with an honesty and a vulnerability that invite participants into a special relationship with the presenter. Small groups become mini-retreat communities where members can safely share details of their lives and their faith with support and without judgment. Optional prayer opportunities to meet with a spiritual director, confessor, and prayer team allow retreatants to express their most heartfelt needs—to be met with love, reconciliation, prayer, and celebration.

Encouraging Openness

Participants might come to the retreat wondering if God moves in their lives at all. They might be seeking a way into what they have been told exists. Often, they are unaware or marginally aware of the traditional stories of the faith, but they can clearly articulate their own life experiences. We prepare young adult team members to give presentations based on their own experiences and their relationships with God. We also pose questions for reflection in order to facilitate dialogue and to assist other young adults as they begin to reflect on their lives. Through the retreat talks, reflection, prayer services, and small-group discussions, participants have opportunities to honestly examine their own experiences.

Overview of Retreat Etiquette

We do not assume that retreatants know appropriate retreat etiquette, so the following is addressed at the onset of the retreat: exposure to silence; respecting one another's physical, psychological, and spiritual space; ground rules for small-group participation; and not using the retreat as a place to pick up dates or customers. Silence and access to a private room are direct answers to the stated need of young adults for a break from the stresses of work, relationships, tasks, and media influences. (See Chapter 6 for more on retreat etiquette.)

Weaving in Elements of Catholic Tradition

While the great majority of Charis retreatants are Roman Catholic, we don't assume that participants are knowledgeable about the Catholic faith. Therefore, we explain what might be familiar (such as a teaching Mass or reconciliation service), introduce in a creative way what is less likely to be familiar (the rosary, adoration of the Blessed Sacrament, *lectio divina*, movement prayer), and lead participants through what might be a completely unfamiliar tradition such as contemplation on Scripture. Storytelling and prayers of imagination or contemplation, especially those based on Gospel stories, link participants to a larger community while engaging those who have been raised on appeals to the senses.

Charis retreats are based heavily on the Spiritual Exercises and apply other values central to the Jesuit tradition, such as the *examen*. The Seekers' Retreat is geared to those who are not yet ready to experience the first week of the Spiritual Exercises. These young adults may or may not have identified their experiences as religious or spiritual; they may or may not have reflected on where God has moved in their lives or in what they desire. Young adults are often eager to tell their own stories. Teaching them to reflect and then teaching them the *examen* is a simple and effective way to help them learn to identify the Spirit's presence with them throughout their day. It connects their "real lives" with their relationship with God. It connects their story with that of Ignatius and with those who have prayed the *examen* through the ages, and it unites them to the larger traditions of Catholic spirituality. This is helpful for those who often say that they have to make up their spirituality as they go or that they have difficulty determining what a fulfilling spiritual practice is and what an empty one is. They might not have learned ways to pray other than those taught to them as children.

Participants also might come weighing major life decisions about their careers, vocations, relationships, and more. They often feel alone and ill-equipped to make such decisions and wonder where God is, or what God's will is, when they make such choices. As tools for making decisions, we introduce prayer and simple reflection exercises as well as Ignatian discernment methods.

Resources for Growth and Healing

Nearly all retreat centers have libraries with spiritual or catechetical reading materials. Charis has found that participants often take advantage of these resources by staying up into the wee hours to read about a saint, hero, or spiritual practice. We have heard many times about how a book, passage, or life event of a figure has fostered a retreatant's growth. Finally, we make available literature that pertains to volunteer opportunities, vocations from local religious communities, young adult gatherings in the area, and parishes that welcome those in their twenties and thirties.

● ● ● ● ● ● ● ● ● ● ● ● ● ● ● ● ● ●

Participants might come weighing major life decisions about their careers, vocations, relationships, and more.

● ●

Spiritual Directors and Pastoral Counselors

Each Charis team has at least one trained spiritual director and often a pastoral counselor. While on retreat, participants often address the areas of brokenness, resistance, and sin in their lives. It is essential to have spiritual directors and counselors who can nurture participants while they move through the pain and try to find healing. Good, compassionate, and positive confessors who celebrate the participant's reconciliation through the sacrament of reconciliation can draw the person not only closer to God and to the retreat community but also more fully into the Catholic community. Having at least one confessor or team member from the Builder Generation (born between 1927 and 1945) has served both the team and participants well.

Encouraging Participation

The emphasis on individual choice during the retreats encourages participation without pressure. We have found that retreatants nearly always attend all the scheduled activities (illness, extreme fatigue, and turmoil roused by confronting brokenness are the usual exceptions) because they want to hear a presenter or see how their group is unfolding. But retreatants are always offered the choice of saying, "No, I am more in need of spiritual direction (or rest or quiet time alone with God) than the next Mass or presenter's talk." The Saturday-afternoon break in the program allows for rest and for optional segments such as experiencing a new prayer form, a walk in the woods, or a Q&A session about Catholic teachings. A variety of options are offered to meet some of the individual needs or interests of participants.

Charis's Response

Today's young adults crave intimacy, community, time away, reflection, a break from stress, spiritual and religious guidance, and a connection to something larger than themselves. In evaluation after evaluation, our participants have placed a high value on having time to reflect, getting opportunities to share their faith and experiences with peers, and hearing presentations by peers. They have also made it clear that they seek to pray creatively, receive the sacraments of reconciliation and the Eucharist in a retreat setting, make sense of the tradition through explanations in contemporary language, and speak one-on-one with a spiritual guide. Through our structure, sensitivity to culture, and foundation in Ignatian spirituality, Charis retreats are designed to meet the spiritual needs of adults in their twenties and thirties.

Charis also aims to help our constituents recognize the movement of the Holy Spirit in their lives. We are preparing young adults to take responsibility for their own spiritual journey with God and to be active in their faith. We are empowering them to be leaders in their faith communities, which may include small groups, parishes, and service programs. We are providing tools for discernment at a time in their lives when they are facing—perhaps for the first time—serious adult decisions that will affect their career, family, and future.

We have heard many stories of spiritual growth, healing, the conversion of lives, and the development or strengthening of relationships. These relationships have been between individuals, between individuals and God, and between individuals and faith communities.

Let's face it: The Catholic Church (along with other mainline denominations) is not always supportive of young adults. This is reflected in church attendance and membership. Charis is helping to build a bridge between the world of young adults and the Catholic faith community. We hope that the result is a lifelong engagement that extends from generation to generation. &

CHAPTER 2

Before You Begin: Preparing for Success

Bringing the Charis retreat program to a new city or region is an exciting and challenging venture. In a way, the effort mirrors the work of famed missionaries such as St. Francis Xavier, St. Katharine Drexel, Blessed Mother Teresa of Calcutta, and Bartolomé de las Casas. These great men and women set out to work for the reign of God in new places. They brought a different face of God to new lands, and at the same time, found God already awaiting them in the persons and cultures they encountered. As she worked with "the poorest of the poor" in Calcutta's streets, Mother Teresa said she found "Christ in a very distressing disguise."

Getting the Lay of the Land

The parallels are clear in ministry with today's Catholic young adults. Like missionaries past and present, those who bring Charis retreats to a new area must first spend time studying and exploring the makeup of the region and its Catholic young adults. Is it a fast-paced and sophisticated urban area? Is it a small or medium-sized town where traditional values prevail? Is the region primarily prosperous or depressed? How much diversity of race, ethnicity, language, and socioeconomic status exists?

All these factors weigh into the way Charis is promoted and tailored for a region.

In addition to the overall culture of a region, Charis leaders should consider the uniqueness of the local church. Local churches are like people: Some things are common across the board, but each has a distinct personality, flavor, and way of doing things. For example, in some southern areas where less than two percent of the population is Catholic, the community can be tightly knit even if the spiritual growth opportunities are limited. By contrast, some cities have a Catholic church on every block, as well as retreat centers, Catholic colleges, and motherhouses of religious orders. Additionally, depending on the diocese, the predominant expression of faith may or may not be a traditional one. Finally, leaders should note whether the church in a given area reflects the growing multicultural reality of our nation.

After assessing an area and its Catholic church, leaders should also examine the specific Catholic young adult population and the state of young adult ministry in the diocese. In Chicago, for example, many young adults have populated certain areas of the city and have revitalized several urban parishes. Young adults make up the majority of the membership in these parishes, so a new young adult ministry might begin there and then branch out. This strategy, however, would be hard to duplicate in a rural area where young adults are spread out across the region. There, a church-bulletin announcement is a good way to reach young adults because the bulletin is akin to a local newspaper that everyone reads. Elsewhere, a bulletin announcement might be far less effective.

Once leaders have studied the nature of the area, the church, and the young adults, the next task is to determine what young adult ministry exists in the area and what program needs to be established. The first question is whether there is a diocesan office of young adult ministry. If so, this office could be an invaluable source of information about the demographics and needs, as well as a potential aid in getting the Charis program up and running.

The second question focuses on young adults themselves: Who is being served, and who is not? In one city, for example, spiritual development opportunities were abundant for those who embraced traditional and devotional expressions of faith. At the same time, few programs served people from mainstream parishes or those oriented to Christian service.

In a different city, the opposite was true. In each of these cases, Charis began by targeting the population and the niche that was not being served. At the same time, we welcomed all and expanded the prayer and spiritual development opportunities across a broad spectrum.

Similarly, Charis might initially fill a ministry gap for singles, married couples, recent college graduates, or people in their thirties. Whatever initial target audience or niche is chosen, however, the ultimate goal for Charis—as for the church itself—is to spread a wide tent, embracing a vast range of spiritualities, ages, lifestyles, and ethnicities. Although it takes effort to create such a tent and to anchor it, some of our most powerful retreats have come as a result of people meeting and sharing their differences with one another. Charis hopes to mirror the James Joyce phrase that aptly describes the Catholic Church: "Here comes everybody!"[1]

> Once leaders have the lay of the land, there is no shortage of ways that Charis can be tailored to fit the ministerial needs that exist.

All that said, on occasion we have chosen to offer retreats solely for men or for women, or for members of one parish or ethnicity. Although these retreats tend to draw smaller crowds than those targeted to wider audiences, specialized retreats do offer unique gifts. A great deal of intimacy and depth can be achieved in a group of all women, all men, or members mostly from one parish or ethnicity. The common ground is more immediate, with less need to translate one's experience across differences. Furthermore, such homogenous experiences can serve as a safe first step that may lead participants into broader-based Charis programs.

Clearly, once leaders have the lay of the land, there is no shortage of ways that Charis can be tailored to fit the many ministerial needs that exist. In evaluating these needs, leaders should also pay attention to the resources available (retreat houses, service-project opportunities, financial assistance, and so on). Among these resources are the leaders' own gifts and areas of interest. "The place God calls you to," says theologian Frederick Buechner, "is the place where your deep gladness and the world's deep hunger meet."[2] Young adult needs in any area are usually many and varied, so Charis leaders are well suited to dream and to consider the areas of a Charis program that excite them most.

Developing a Base of Support

In addition to taking into account the nature of the area and the young adult ministries available, potential Charis leaders should also seek to build relationships with those who might be key stakeholders in and supporters of such a program. These can include

- diocesan young adult ministry offices, which often exist as part of the youth ministry, family life, or religious-education offices;
- diocesan offices for multicultural ministry;
- alumni offices of local Jesuit and other Catholic high schools and colleges;
- diocesan school offices that seek to offer ministry to their young teachers;
- pastoral staffs of the most young adult-friendly parishes;
- directors of local retreat centers;
- leaders of Catholic singles and young adult groups;
- vocation ministers of religious congregations;
- military chaplains if there is a base in the area; and
- priests, religious, and lay ministers who are themselves young adults.

In small dioceses, leaders may find it advantageous to meet directly with the local bishop and to introduce him to the new program. In large dioceses, bishops may prefer that leaders meet with those who are in charge of young adult ministry.

These contacts can be invaluable sources of information about young adults in the area, what they need, and how best to reach them. Additionally, these stakeholders can utilize their networks of young adult contacts and resources to publicize Charis, such as e-mail and mailing lists, bulletins, diocesan newspapers, and communication offices. Finally, some of these contacts may themselves be interested in helping. They may suggest others or be able to identify young adult leaders to help promote Charis or to serve on the initial retreat teams. These contacts might also be willing to serve as or to identify others to serve as confessors, spiritual directors, or pastoral counselors on Charis retreats.

When Charis was initiated in Cincinnati, the diocesan young adult ministry was just beginning as a one-person office. This person welcomed the opportunity to launch diocesan young adult ministry by partnering with Charis in order to get both off the ground at the same time. Other diocesan young adult programs grew from Charis's foundation. In addition, a Jesuit university and several Catholic high schools in Cincinnati sent Charis brochures and invitation letters to their young adult alumni. Finally, the Catholic Schools Office sent Charis promotional materials to all the principals to give to their younger teachers. All these stakeholders in young adult ministry welcomed the opportunity to partner with Charis while advancing their own missions.

Starting Small and Building Up

Leaders in cities such as Indianapolis have chosen to start Charis programming with short events and to gradually build up to offering a weekend retreat. The advantage of shorter events is that they enable busy young adults to try Charis without investing an entire weekend. Since Charis's inception less than a decade ago, we have noticed that young adults have grown busier and busier. Therefore, they are more reluctant to commit an entire weekend to an unfamiliar experience. Additionally, shorter events can attract a broader base of retreatants, since they are more compatible with the schedules of parents and those who work on weekends.

Shortened forms of Charis have included days of prayer, Friday-night-to-Saturday-afternoon events, and evening gatherings. Another short Charis experience is the afternoon mini-retreat. In Cleveland, the Charis mini-retreat has served as the more reflective track of the annual statewide young adult conference. A Charis afternoon could also serve as a breakout session for young adults at a multigenerational conference. (See Chapter 10 for a detailed description of shortened and alternative forms of Charis events, such as days of prayer and mini-retreats.)

Bold and Basic Promotional Methods

Once the landscape is explored and key contacts have been developed, the possible methods for promoting Charis are limited only by the imagination and budget of those seeking to get the word out. Ideally, we would hire an airplane to fly a Charis banner over the Ohio State-Michigan football game, but budgetary constraints rule that out. The point is this: Think outside the box. At the same time, however, think *inside* the box. Tried and true promotional methods have proved successful, but reaching new generations also requires bold and new approaches.

Thinking inside the box means utilizing familiar methods of promoting church activities: announcements in church bulletins and at Sunday Mass; postings in the calendar section of the local newspaper; and press releases sent to the Catholic newspaper. Although few young adults themselves may read the bulletin, their parents, grandparents, and associates do. Many Charis attendees have come after a nudge from a relative. One executive even convinced and paid for his young administrative assistant to attend.

Other familiar methods include mailing letters of invitation and brochures to various mailing lists, posting brochures in church vestibules and campus bulletin boards, and sending news releases. (See the retreat resource books for examples of promotional materials.)

Even these standard promotional methods can be enhanced by fresh approaches. Young adults have been the targets of marketing since they were in kindergarten. Written materials, therefore, should not simply announce a retreat in passive or "churchy" language: "Retreat will be held January 14–16 at St. Martin's Retreat Center. Silence will be observed, and sacramental reconciliation will be provided."

Instead, promotional materials should name and address a young adult need and should indicate what the retreat will offer. The message should be inviting, appealing, and fresh. An example is on the following page.

Because of confusion about the meaning of the phrase *young adult*, Charis and other young adult events should always spell out specifically whom the event is for. We have found that many assume that *young adult* means "youth," so age range must be given in order to avoid drawing an all-teen audience. Others assume that *young adult* is synonymous with *single*, so married people may assume they are not welcome. The easiest way to quell confusion is to spell out the demographic you are seeking to attract.

Charis Young Adult Retreat
Had enough of the winter blues? Come take the chill off with a Charis Retreat, for single and married men and women in their twenties and thirties, January 26–28 at Maryhill Retreat Center. Meet new friends around the fireplace, take a quiet walk in the woods, celebrate lively liturgy, learn new ways to pray. Cost for the weekend, including room and board is $150; financial assistance is available. Contact (name) at (phone) or (e-mail). Visit www.CharisMinistries.org for more information.

Visual promotion can be as important as the written word. In Cincinnati, some of our first contacts were young adult graphic designers who were anxious to assist our ministry at no charge. If your budget allows for it, professional, multicolored advertising materials can win particular attention, especially for the first couple of retreats. But even inexpensive brochures can feature appealing graphics, drawings, and photos. Include photos of the audience if you are trying to draw young adult men and women of various races. Unless your retreat center is as architecturally interesting as the Taj Mahal, showing photos of the buildings by themselves will not engage your audience. We have found that eye-catching graphics and humorous but not irreverent language are especially effective.

More Fresh Approaches

In addition to the methods noted above, Charis has explored other ways to promote its events. These methods are described in the following sections.

Arts or Business Publications

Place ads in a local arts paper or downtown business journal, both of which are read by young adults who may not have a parish connection.

Radio

Announcements on popular radio stations can reach large audiences.

Business Cards

Consider creating business cards announcing the next Charis event, including contact information and a Web address. The cards can be handed out after conversations with people at parties, bars, health clubs, street festivals, or marathons. Of course, it is important that the people who give out the cards take care not to pressure anyone and not to engage in indiscriminate solicitation. Otherwise, this method could turn people off, run afoul of an establishment's rules, and reflect poorly on Charis.

Web Sites

Web sites are an essential means of communication with young adults. Create a Web site or at least a Web page on another site such as a diocesan office, retreat center, or Jesuit school. As with brochures, the site should offer the essential information (event, dates, place, time, cost, contact information) in an attractive and inviting format, with fresh language, photos, and graphics. Frequently changing the display will get people in the habit of checking the site regularly. The Web site should be accessible to those with lower-end computers. Any information contained on pop-up screens should also be available on the Web page itself, since many people use pop-up controls. Charis announcements should be listed on other sites such as the diocesan site and the host retreat center's site. The Paulist Fathers run a national Catholic young adult Web site that lists upcoming events around the country as well as other great resources: www.BustedHalo.com.

E-mail

E-mail is capable of reaching a huge contingent of people without the costs of postage or the harm to trees. Here are the do's (and one don't) of e-mail promotion of Charis events:

- Do continually grow and update your database of e-mail addresses. Invite those who visit the Charis Web site or receive promotional materials to join the Charis e-mail list.

- Do send out Charis announcements via e-mail. Use fresh, inviting language that conveys information and piques interest.

- Do provide the information as plain text without hyperlinks in the body of the e-mail for those with lower-end computers or who receive e-mail via cell phone or PDA. You can jazz up the same material in attachments if you want to.

- Do send out Charis e-mails with regularity. In our experience, people appreciate a monthly announcement of events; this reminds everyone that Charis is alive and offering opportunities. Occasional mid-month reminders of events are also acceptable. Realize, however, that recipients often receive a high volume of e-mail, so less is more. Sending out too many e-mails can result in more requests to be removed from the list.

- Do list instructions at the bottom of each e-mail for recipients to unsubscribe from the list. This ability to opt out is required by many Internet service providers, and it makes sense. Make removal from the list as easy as possible. For example, invite the recipient to hit *reply,* type *unsubscribe* in the subject line, and hit *send.*

- Do be aware that use of the word *adult* in the subject line or even in the body of the e-mail will cause some e-mail systems to reject the e-mail because of controls rejecting all adult content. Since *young adult* is such an integral part of the promotional language, this can be problematic. One suggestion is to focus on the topic in the subject line (as in Spring and Summer Retreats) rather than the audience (as in Young Adult Retreats). To avoid stating *young adult,* you can note in the body of the e-mail the age range of the audience (men and women in their twenties and thirties).

- Do provide all the highlights for your announcements at the beginning of the e-mail. This allows recipients to scan quickly and determine what interests them most. Make your headlines enticing so that people want to keep reading. Examples: *Come Chill Out at the Winter Charis Retreat—January 26–28; Why Would Anyone Choose to Be Catholic? Find out February 7–9; Don't Let the Fire Burn Out! Charis Reunion March 9–11.*

- Don't send e-mail in such a way that everyone's address is visible to everyone else. This violates people's privacy, invites co-opting of the list for other purposes, and risks someone hitting *reply all* and aggravating everyone else. One way to protect the privacy of the list is to send the e-mail to yourself and blind carbon copy (BCC) everyone else on the list.

House Parties

Leaders in Chicago found fun and low-budget ways to promote Charis before the retreats ever started. Young adults are accustomed to being invited to marketing parties for everything from kitchen appliances to makeup to home decor. Charis house parties draw on the same concept, using in-home hospitality to expose friends and family to an opportunity. Charis house parties also continue our ancient faith tradition of gathering friends and families into our homes for worship—the prevailing practice when the Acts of the Apostles was written.

A young adult hosts the Charis house party, supplying a meal or refreshments for the friends he or she has invited. Charis leaders give a presentation about the retreat, lead prayer, and engage the group in authentic conversation by relating Charis themes to the guests' own lives. The evening can become a microcosm of a Charis retreat, with guests making connections beyond the superficial and experiencing a taste of the fun, engagement, and depth that a whole weekend might offer. Some guests will likely leave the party resolved to make a retreat and, perhaps, invite friends. House parties can generate enthusiasm, draw participants, and even surface potential team members.

Focus Groups

Cincinnati leaders initiated Charis through a concept similar to house parties: focus groups. The leaders identified and invited some fifteen to twenty young adult leaders in the area (parish youth/young adult ministers, organization leaders, corporate executives, teachers, and so on) to spend an evening at the retreat center where a Charis program was scheduled. After socializing over pizza and soft drinks, the leaders engaged the group in creative prayer and gave an overview of Charis, including its history and the model itself.

The participants helped determine the nature of Charis (whether it should be coed or not) and developed a plan for how to spread the word in the area. Then participants were invited to stand by one of the signs hanging around the room that most attracted them. The signs named various themes of Charis. Six single women laughed when they found themselves gathered under the *Deepest Desires* sign. A priest and a young man huddled in conversation beneath *Suffering, Healing, and Hope.* In those groups, participants talked with one another about what aspect of that topic drew them, and what they might hope to gain from a larger retreat addressing that theme. The evening concluded with most participants making a commitment to advance Charis, followed by a group blessing. In Cincinnati, two such focus groups and other promotional efforts yielded a full retreat house with a waiting list for the first several Charis retreats.

Cost and Resources

Price is a key element that young adults consider when deciding whether or not to make a Charis retreat. Setting the price is a difficult task that raises a number of considerations:

- drawing participants to invest their money and time in Charis, especially on the first few retreats;

- ensuring that the retreat program eventually pays for itself;

- setting prices consistent with similar programs in the region;

- eliminating finance as a barrier to participation;

- cultivating donations, grants, and other sources of financial aid; and

- providing for the expenses of the young adult team, who are generally not paid but stay at the retreat center and partake in the meals.

How these considerations play out may vary depending on the area. For example, some retreat centers may subsidize the first several Charis retreats to attract a new and young clientele and to get the program off to a good start. Leaders who don't have an independent budget might charge a little more than cost and then use the excess to subsidize those for whom price is an obstacle. Others are simply unable to offer financial assistance, especially when the initial retreats are small. Regardless of how these issues are resolved (and they might be worked out through trial and error over time), the important thing is to recognize that cost is an integral element in promoting and growing Charis in a new area.

Timing and Deadlines

Avoid unfriendly deadlines and giving up too soon. This observation is not meant to be offensive or insulting to young adults, but many, if not most, seem to register just prior to deadlines. There are valid reasons for this (overcommitment, scheduling conflicts, keeping options open), but it remains a reality. Responding to this reality calls for patience, flexibility, and creativity.

Some leaders have advertised rewards such as T-shirts for the first ten people who sign up. Others

> It is still essential to get events onto people's calendars as soon as possible, but don't cancel events or firm up your expectations too soon.

have offered financial incentives, with prices increasing the closer to the event a person registers. Leaders and teams may have to be flexible and realize that many people may register the day before or even the day of an event. A sure way to sabotage a Charis program is to impose deadlines drawn from the norms of earlier generations, such as requiring registration a month in advance or canceling the event because too few are signed up two weeks ahead. Although there will always be early birds, leaders should take into account varying generational norms for registration.

This does not mean that leaders should wait until the last minute to promote events. It is still essential to get them onto people's crowded calendars as soon as possible and to maximize their opportunities to attend. But don't cancel events or firm up your expectations too soon.

Racial and Ethnic Diversity

Among the richest experiences of Charis have been retreats that combined African American, Asian American, European American, and Hispanic American participation. Most of today's young adults have experienced multiculturalism in several aspects of their lives: schools, workplaces, recreational and cultural activities. Many have traveled and/or studied internationally. Therefore, a substantial number of young adults have come to expect diversity in their gatherings, and they are surprised and often disappointed when it is lacking.

In church matters, however, multicultural participation does not happen so smoothly and seamlessly. Rather, Sunday worship services are often quite segregated. To offset this tendency toward homogenous religious events, leaders must make a particular effort to introduce and ground Charis in the various Catholic racial and ethnic communities. Leaders can achieve cultural diversity in Charis through

- learning from and building relationships in various racial and ethnic communities;

- developing promotional materials that reflect diversity; and

- incorporating elements of cultural diversity into the retreat itself.

Charis leaders faced the challenge of bringing the program to Cincinnati during a season when racial tensions erupted into violence and unrest. At that time, one of the leaders developing Charis was Tim Hipskind, S.J., a pastoral minister living, working, and worshipping in an African American community. Fr. Tim challenged all of us promoting Charis to realize that the church's body of knowledge about young adults was limited. Most of the research was focused on European American young adults, some was focused on Hispanic Americans, and little was focused on African Americans and other racial and ethnic communities. We found that some research and knowledge holds true across the board, but a lot of it does not. Those developing Charis should therefore come as pilgrims to each racial or ethnic community they approach, seeking to learn the wisdom that these communities offer.

Fr. Tim's contacts in Cincinnati's African American community proved invaluable, as did the relationship Charis cultivated with the archdiocesan Office of African American Ministries. Fr. Tim and other Charis leaders recruited young adults in urban parishes to assist with promotion. Together they handed out brochures in these churches, announced Charis events at Masses, and invited participation. Additionally, the leaders invited a cross section of young adults from urban parishes to their focus session to help design Charis and to decide how Charis could best meet multicultural needs. Furthermore, because the African American community is highly relational, in-person contact and personal invitations proved far more effective than e-mail or mass mailings.

The lesson is clear. In order to promote Charis in diverse communities, it is important to take the time to make key contacts and build relationships within those communities. Charis leaders also must learn about the community itself and the best ways of communicating and inviting participation and leadership. Because of the time and energy this takes, it may only be possible to focus on one community at a time.

In addition to making connections, Charis leaders should also ensure that promotional materials reflect a multicultural reality. The photos in brochures and on the Web site should include multiple ethnicities. Some of the Web site and some brochures or parts of brochures could be in Spanish if it is feasible to offer bilingual or Spanish-speaking Charis events.

> A multicultural effort requires Charis leaders to be flexible and to take risks.

Furthermore, the retreat team should solidly reflect diversity. If possible, the team should include several members of the same racial or ethnic community, as well as an older pastoral minister or priest from that community. If there is only one African American team member, for example, there is a great risk that he or she could feel pressured to take sole responsibility for outreach to all the African American retreatants or be put on the spot to answer all race questions that arise. This is a heavy burden that should be avoided.

The retreat itself should also contain elements of the various cultures represented. One of the riches of Cincinnati's Charis program is the gospel choir from a predominantly African American parish that provides the music for Saturday night's prayer service. Many young adult choir members who have not participated in Charis have nonetheless contributed by leading the assembly in song at the retreats. Other liturgical music might be sung in Spanish, or readings and prayers might be offered in a mix of English and Korean, Vietnamese, or Polish. Ethnic foods could be provided or Latin dancing taught at the social as a means of celebrating the gifts of the various cultures represented. Again, creativity knows no bounds in this area.

Finally, a multicultural effort requires Charis leaders to be flexible and to take risks. In Cincinnati, we were not sure if the European American young adults would fully appreciate the gospel music incorporated into our Saturday-night prayer. But they loved it! (This was a good lesson for the baby boomer pastoral ministers developing Charis: The boomer generation generally has less experience with diversity in church settings and is probably less open to it than younger generations are.)

The diversity among team members in Cincinnati challenged us to face some of our assumptions about how things have to be done. For instance, do talks have to be written out in advance? Can they be interactive instead of monologues? We have had to wade into these waters and learn by trying. It helps to try things in advance in other settings or at team meetings. It also helps to be flexible with the structure of the retreat itself; maybe a twenty-five-minute presentation could become a shorter liturgical reflection.

Flexibility with where and how Charis events take place is also important. Some of the team preparation or the Charis events themselves might take place on-site at urban or minority parishes, giving young adults wide exposure to the many faces of Catholicism in their communities. Charis events might also be designed primarily with and for young adults from one or more churches, especially when language is a barrier. The creative possibilities are endless.

In sum, the lesson for welcoming diversity in Charis events is this: Be open!

Conclusion

In short, just as the missionaries of past and present found a variety of ways to work toward the reign of God in new places and new cultures, so Charis leaders are taking numerous approaches to bringing this particular face of God to young adults in new areas. Five steps are especially helpful in advancing the Charis mission:

1. Assess what is available for Catholic young adults in a particular area, and what they most need right now.

2. Begin to build relationships with key stakeholders in young adult ministry.
3. Offer young adults a chance to meet Charis leaders and to experience a taste of what Charis offers.
4. Develop and distribute promotional materials, including online materials.
5. Consider starting small and building from there. This doesn't mean you can't dream big, but even the pyramids were built stone by stone from the ground up.

Designing the Model: Movements of a Charis Retreat

For any Charis retreat, the aim is to lead the retreatant from welcomed, interested newcomer to an adult who can express his or her faith. The power of Charis retreats lies in the strength of peer witness and in the ability of young adults to articulate—through their faith journeys—that they struggle and they believe.

Over the course of the program, which ideally is a weekend but may be shorter, the aim is to build an atmosphere of trust in which young adults can name their religious experiences and be challenged to grow by peer leaders who articulate their own experiences. It is the job of the team and the purpose of the retreats to provide for the retreatant a safe space to meet Christ and a space where that encounter may be shared with other struggling believers.

Structure

Charis retreats are composed of "building blocks," meaning that retreatants are eased gradually into their experience. As the retreat unfolds, they go deeper and deeper into their spiritual lives. The blocks consist of peer presentations (talks), periods of silent individual reflection, and small-group sharing. In addition, opportunities are offered for communal prayer and for individual spiritual direction. On pages 38–39 is a basic outline of a Charis retreat. Below are some details about the contents of each block. (See subsequent chapters for more information.)

> Visit **www.CharisRetreats.org** to download and customize materials for the specific blocks of a retreat.

Building Blocks for Retreat Talks

Presentations are talks given by young adult team members who have prepared thoroughly with the pastoral staff. The talks are essentially theological reflections that reveal the presenters' integration of their lives and their religious experiences with Scripture and tradition. The presentations begin and end with a song or video that pertains to the topic.

In their talks, the presenters recall both their struggles with faith and their moments of grace. The talks also answer a number of questions that will be submitted to the retreatants for their consideration during the silent/individual reflection period that follows. (See Chapter 5 for a complete discussion on talks and talk preparation.)

Silent or Individual Reflection

Following most of the talks is a period of silence when retreatants and team members may reflect on and answer (in prayer or in a journal) the questions offered by the presenter. The periods may be as short as thirty minutes (after the first presentation) or as long as sixty minutes (late in the retreat). The retreat space—including the conference room, the chapel, and the sleeping rooms—remains silent during this period to facilitate prayerful reflection. To help retreatants who might not be comfortable with total silence, quiet instrumental music may be played in a common space such as the chapel or conference room.

Small Groups

At the end of the silent reflection period, retreatants are invited to gather with five, six, or seven of their peers to share as much of their reflections as they feel comfortable. The small groups are essentially theological reflection groups facilitated by a trained peer team member. The small group acts as a retreat-within-a-retreat, a place where retreatants may experience intimacy and community. It is the place where the retreatant may, perhaps for the first time, honestly and safely name his or her faith struggles. He or she can openly praise God and proclaim thanks for blessings and moments of grace discovered during the reflection or during a meaningful time of discovery in his or her life. Because of the intimacy of the topics shared in the group, it is essential that group facilitators be well trained and that guidelines such as confidentiality and no "J.A.B.-ing" (*J*udging, *A*dvice Giving, or *B*laming) are maintained. (See Chapter 7 for more on small groups and small-group training.)

Sample Charis Retreat Schedule

Friday (First Block)

- Registration
- Table blessing, dinner, introductions, welcome
- Prologue: Why are you here?
- First presentation
- Personal activity (silence)
- Small-group sharing
- Brief break
- Meditation
- Retire

Saturday (Second—Fourth Blocks)

Second Block

- Breakfast
- Prayer
- Announcements
- Second presentation
- Personal activity (silence)
- Small-group sharing
- Lunch, free time, individual conferences (optional)

Prayer and Spiritual Direction

Over the course of the Charis weekend retreat, there are multiple opportunities to experience traditional forms of prayer. Each retreat provides experiences of evening and morning prayer, Mass, the sacrament of reconciliation, intercessory prayer, and guided-imagery prayer. In addition, the *examen*, Ignatian contemplation, adoration of the Blessed Sacrament, movement prayer, the rosary, and other prayers may be offered. We encourage the pastoral staff to introduce or lead prayer forms according to interest and expertise. The prayer forms should not only be led but also

Third Block

- Third presentation
- Personal activity (silence)
- Small-group sharing
- Short break
- Liturgy
- Dinner

Fourth Block

- Fourth presentation
- Personal activity (silence)
- Small-group sharing
- Short break
- Celebration of sacrament of reconciliation
- Retire, social gathering (optional), or individual conferences (optional)

Sunday (Fifth Block)

- Breakfast
- Fifth presentation
- Personal activity (silence)
- Small-group sharing
- Short break
- Liturgy, missioning
- Sharing and lunch
- Departure

explained and taught to the young adult retreatants.

We also encourage those using this guide to offer the option of one-on-one spiritual direction for retreatants. Charis retreats in Cincinnati and Chicago always have at least two trained spiritual directors available to meet during individual-reflection times, free periods such as Saturday afternoon of the full-weekend Seekers' Retreat, and during the Saturday-evening prayer service. In Cincinnati, vocations directors for religious communities are often invited to serve in this important role. We strongly recommend that there be a balance of male and female directors if possible. (See Chapter 8 for detailed suggestions for conducting prayer and providing spiritual direction.)

Retreat Dynamics

The Charis retreat is designed on the assumption that this will be the first retreat for many of the participants. Apart from attending Mass, it may be participants' first time engaging in a specifically religious practice, intentionally choosing to open themselves to God's Spirit. We assume that the decision to attend is not a decision made lightly and that the participant may walk in the door with some trepidation, shyness, and even fear of what may happen over the course of the program. Pre-retreat communication from organizers should take the edge off these feelings. Even so, the assumption is that at the beginning of the retreat, the participant may arrive feeling awkward and nervous.

For that reason—and to ensure that the retreatants' enthusiasm and a commitment to taking faith and religious practice to a new level is authentic—the dynamic deliberately builds slowly. The dynamic is outlined below, based on a Friday-evening through Sunday-afternoon weekend retreat, though the dynamic is similar if the program is abbreviated for pastoral or financial reasons.

1. Friday Night: Getting Comfortable

Friday night is spent easing into the retreat. It is a time of hospitality, introduction, and overview. (The dynamic outlined below is discussed more thoroughly in Chapter 6.)

Welcome and Social

- Team members and/or other volunteers greet each participant at the entrance to the retreat facility.

- Participants receive retreat materials and make final registration and payment.

- Participants are invited to dinner (if provided) and are shown their rooms to settle in.

- The team and participants introduce themselves at dinner or at a welcome session.

- There may also be an icebreaker prior to the official start of the retreat for team members and retreatants to learn names and get comfortable with one another.

Another introductory element comes during the first talk on Friday evening. Participants are introduced to an "entry-level" reflection on their own lives. Then they are invited to share the fruits of their reflection during the first small-group gathering.

Establishing Ground Rules After dinner and before the first talk and small-group gathering, the entire group gathers in a conference room (or chapel arranged for talks) to listen to a presentation by the team. The presentation provides a foundation for the retreat. It

- introduces prayer as a central component;
- suggests why one might come on retreat;

- explains the philosophy and theology underlying the Charis retreat;

- outlines the format and various elements of the retreat;

- provides an overview of house logistics; and

- introduces the small-group guidelines.

 See Chapter 4 of the retreat resource books and Chapter 4 of this guide for details and suggestions on team preparation.

This part of the retreat is focused on establishing behavioral guidelines and expectations for the team and participants. Because we want participants to feel safe to pray and to express their feelings and thoughts about their relationship with God, we set guidelines about confidentiality, appropriate sharing, and social behaviors. Chapter 6 covers these guidelines in more detail. Guidelines for small-group sharing and behaviors are also outlined in this session. (See Chapter 7 for more on small-group guidelines.)

Getting Rest The Friday-evening schedule is full, but the pace and content of the formal periods—talk, reflection, sharing—are designed to be slow, restful, and relaxing. Each of the formal periods is shortest on Friday evening, and prayer is meant to help the participants review the evening and relax almost to the point of sleep. The evening ends early so that all may have enough rest to hear the Lord's voice the remainder of the weekend.

2. Saturday Day: Entering More Deeply

Saturday morning and afternoon of the retreat are designed to gradually lead the retreatant more deeply into his or her own experience both of life and of the Holy. After morning prayer, a team member gives a talk about what is important to young adults: relationships, commitments, values, and priorities. The team member emphasizes our relationship with God, our commitment to a faith community, and the importance of practicing our faith in daily life. Retreatants are invited to longer periods of personal reflection on topics important to their own lives and to share their reflections with the small group. The talk that follows lunch invites the retreatant to go deeper still, into specifically spiritual territory. It addresses prayer and discernment and invites retreatants to apply them to everyday life. In Chicago, for example, various forms of prayer are reviewed. The *examen* of St. Ignatius is introduced as a particularly effective method of prayer and discernment for young adults. The reflection and sharing time may lead into a eucharistic liturgy before dinner.

The team will decide on its own whether to celebrate Mass on Saturday, considering the circumstances and practices of participants. Some retreats have no Saturday Mass. Others celebrate Mass early in the morning. Still others schedule Mass before lunch or dinner. We encourage pastoral sensitivity for those conducting Charis retreats: Do what best fits the schedule, interests, and practices of the retreatants and the team. We recommend that the Saturday Mass, if celebrated, take place no later than immediately before the evening meal.

Hitting Your Stride As the second day progresses, the talk-reflection–small-group dynamic becomes routine. Participants are less anxious about where they're supposed to be and can enter into the repeated processes of listening, reflecting, sharing, and prayer. This "retreat stride" comes by lunchtime for many participants, when they can have relaxed social conversations over a good meal, followed by a lengthy break when they can continue to reflect, journal, pray, nap, walk the grounds, swim, or enjoy the outdoors. Retreatants are usually able to go deeper with the afternoon and evening topics after becoming relaxed and hitting their stride.

Praying Together and Learning New Ways to Pray An exciting part of Saturday is the opportunity for young adults to experience prayer. While many come with a history of rote prayer or Sunday worship, few have experienced the *examen,* Ignatian contemplation, guided meditations, healing prayer, or even the rosary, at least as adults. Inviting young adults to pray together, and especially to lead prayer (with guidance), allows them to relate to one another and to the Trinity in new ways. It allows them to model leadership and to realize that a relationship with God is just that—a living, growing, changing partnership of love between oneself and another. The talks and formal prayer experiences throughout Saturday emphasize this living relationship. Often, young adults are surprised to hear that prayer consists of more than talking to God and that it can incorporate conversation, music, journal writing, or contemplation before the Blessed Sacrament, nature, or an icon. Participating in various prayer forms, including ones they currently use but had not identified as prayer, can be joyous experiences.

Exploring Issues of Concern As participants become more comfortable and enter more deeply into their prayer and experience, issues of concern in their lives often rise to the surface. The repeated periods of silence and the opportunities to explore the joys and sorrows of past experiences can often lead to feelings of vulnerability over past or present wounds, decisions, or actions.

It is critical that the team be aware of this dynamic and that experienced spiritual directors be available for participants to speak with during the silent reflection periods and afternoon break. The director may serve as a

● ● ● ● ● ● ● ● ● ● ● ● ● ● ● ● ●

After a day of reflection, prayer, and celebration, many retreatants enter into the deepest places of their hearts.

● ●

spiritual companion, holding people in prayer as they share the fruits of the retreat. If the areas raised are of a serious psychological, emotional, or psychiatric nature, the retreat director may suggest further direction or the initiation of other supportive relationships or counseling.

3. Saturday Night: The Deepest Places

After a day of reflection, prayer, downtime, and celebration at the Eucharist and at dinner, we have found that many retreatants are usually able to enter into the deepest places of their hearts. They have begun to get to know their souls and perhaps discover evidence that God (or at least love) has been with them in key moments throughout their lives. They have become comfortable with the team, the members of the small group, and the leaders of prayer and direction. Perhaps they have become hungry for more, for an immediate encounter with the Trinity. Saturday evening's format and content seek to offer that contact in a safe, supportive environment.

The Saturday evening talk, which builds on Saturday's liturgy (if offered) and points to Sunday's liturgy, clearly outlines the paschal mystery in the speaker's own life. Participants are carefully and lovingly invited to do the same. Throughout the talk, the reflection period that follows, and the prayer service that replaces small-group sharing, the team takes great pains to provide a safe atmosphere through their actions, words, and physical environment. The speakers who give the Saturday evening talk often reveal areas of great pain or trial in their lives, as well as what or who has given them healing, strength, hope, or an experience of resurrection. Retreatants are then invited to identify the suffering that resulted from their own or someone else's sin and to offer it to Christ.

Conversion, Change, Healing, and Encounter We have found that the invitation we offer into retreatants' own paschal mystery opens them to the experience of conversion—honestly naming the areas of death and sin and rejecting them in order to accept Christ's healing. In the Seekers' Retreat, the retreatants' hearts are open to dark or painful experiences. They hear peers name times when they have been sources of suffering for others, when they have felt God's absence because of death or loss, or when they were damaged by another's sin. Yet hearing the speaker name where God was during or after the experience allows the listener to look for God's fingerprint in his or her own darkest moments.

In the reflection period that follows the talk, retreatants are invited to identify moments of sin and suffering, as well as those of hope, healing, and strength that have come from outside themselves. They may name such moments as encounters with God, and even be led to an immediate encounter through prayer and reflection.

Moving into the Light During the talk and reflection period, and especially in the prayer service that follows the reflection, participants are invited out of the dark moments they identified and into Christ's healing light. In the talk, this is accomplished by naming a moment of hope or healing. A prayer service follows the talk and reflection time, which formally closes the evening. At this service, participants are encouraged to invite Christ directly into their lives through sacrament and prayer.

Light, Sound, and Ritual During reflection and evening prayer, the retreatants' senses are given special attention. Lights are dimmed as retreatants confront areas of pain, healing, and hope. Candles are lit throughout the chapel or worship space for evening prayer. Retreatants are invited to light candles as they move through the dynamic of the evening prayer.

Soft music plays during the reflection period and when retreatants may partake of a variety of prayer options. Musicians may set the atmosphere with songs of hope, strength, and deliverance. For many retreatants, the music provided by talented pastoral musicians and/or well-selected music recordings facilitates movement from places of pain to places of light and healing. For all the participants, sound and light serve to set a warm, safe environment and a reflective or celebratory mood for the Saturday-evening ritual.

In that ritual, participants are invited to communal prayer that includes singing, the proclamation of Scripture, and a homily. They are then invited to partake of any or all of the following: individual confessions with sacramental absolution, private meditation, spiritual direction with a trained minister, and healing prayer. Individual confessions are conducted by priest-directors and guest priests as they are available, usually behind screens or in sacristies, vestries, or confessionals off the chapel. It is important that retreatants also have the opportunity for one-on-one spiritual direction at this time, preferably from both male and female ministers.

> Sound and light serve to set a warm, safe environment and a reflective or celebratory mood for the Saturday-evening ritual.

Participants may also choose to meditate silently in the chapel. Pastoral coordinators may choose to have a fountain of running water (except during Lent), the display of religious icons, or exposition of the Blessed Sacrament in a monstrance as an object of devotion and meditation. As with other prayer forms introduced throughout the weekend, the homily should include catechesis about adoration for those who are not familiar with this devotion.

Finally, healing prayer is offered. Two or three team members sit beside an empty chair where they will offer prayers of healing, hope, reconciliation, or intercession for anyone seeking them.

Charis has made it standard practice in Chicago and Cincinnati to have at least one healing prayer team composed entirely of women. It has been our experience that female retreatants who have been abused or assaulted or who have struggled with relationship or childbearing issues often seek the all-female prayer team.

When retreatants have participated in one, two, or all the prayer options, they are invited to light a taper and place it at the foot of the altar. This is a symbol of their individual prayers and of their readiness to conclude the communal prayer. The ritual signifies healing and hope and defines a time when the issues raised during the retreat are addressed individually and communally and offered to the Lord ritually.

Ethical Responsibilities The Saturday-evening portion of each Charis retreat is often the period of greatest intensity and vulnerability for retreatants. They have been led through their own experiences of life and death and are invited to turn them over to the Lord and to celebrate God's love, grace, and mercy. It is of the utmost importance that professional and volunteer team members be sensitive to this vulnerability. Retreatants should be encouraged to enter into the experience as they are able, and they should not be pushed into their darkest moments, either during the talk, reflection period, or prayer. The pastoral ministers and team must monitor the emotional level and energy of the group and adjust the atmosphere—the lights, the music, length of service—accordingly.

It is important that team members encourage retreatants to enter into the dynamic as the evening progresses and underscore the importance of not distracting other retreatants. Because the retreatant often encounters painful or joyful emotions throughout the evening, the team must be aware that whatever is revealed in healing prayer should be treated as confidential and holy. The entire retreat is holy ground, and at no time is it more holy than during the Saturday-evening prayer service. Confidentiality, sensitivity, genuine love, and support for the retreatants should be demonstrated through respectful speech, demeanor, touch (such as a hand on the shoulder during healing prayer if the retreatant so desires), and prayer.

A final note about ethical responsibilities: Issues often arise during healing prayer that may cause concern among team members. What should be done with a person who is in tears over past abuse, who has recently been abused, or is clearly in need of further counseling? The team member's first responsibility is to be a prayer, to invite the Holy Spirit upon the person for healing and strength—the qualities that team members ask for in their own prayer requests. If areas of concern arise here or in other portions of the retreat, team members are encouraged to suggest that the person speak with a director. A team member could also speak confidentially to the director or pastoral minister. Names are not used unless there is concern that the person might harm self or others.

Why the Ice-Cream Social Matters Following the evening prayer service, the participants and team members are invited to a social gathering. For many, the service will have been an uplifting experience. Maybe they had a confessor who was compassionate and helped them truly celebrate reconciliation. Perhaps through healing prayer, they experienced the comfort that someone will join them in their vulnerability and present their needs to the Lord. Or maybe they received some enlightenment, comfort, strength, or joy during silent contemplation. Finally, if the service ends with joyous music, as we recommend, participants may want to socialize and celebrate with new friends after a period of confronting injuries and sin. In addition to providing that opportunity, the social time also serves as a transition to Sunday morning's focus on light and mission. (We typically offer sweet refreshments such as soft drinks and ice-cream sundaes, as well as non-sugary snacks such as chips, salsa, and pizza. Alcohol is not provided.)

Not all participants will choose to attend the social gathering. Some may remain in private prayer in the chapel, eager to continue in a place where they encountered or are experiencing the Holy. Others may go directly from the service to bed. Because some participants may still be tender from the experience of reflection and prayer, we recommend that a team member or pastoral minister be available for private conversation away from the social gathering.

4. Sunday Morning: Time of Integration

Sunday morning is a time for participants to integrate their experiences. The morning talk pulls together the movements of the retreat and talk themes to present the ultimate topic. In the Seekers' Retreat, the movement is toward helping one to identify his or her deepest desires and to name them as the fundamental desire for God. The entire weekend has been a movement of naming past experiences, values, and relationships. Retreatants have identified their relationship with God through prayer; times when values were not followed or relationships were broken; and

> Spread the news that God is at the center of our desires, that love is the foundation of our lives.

occasions when values, relationships, and desires were named, met, and made new. In the Sunday talk, the speaker names this movement and models the integration of the retreat's dynamic in a thirty-minute reflection. The private reflection and small-group periods allow participants to do the same.

Taking the Retreat into the World Sunday morning is a time for retreatants to name their desire for God and realize that God makes all things new. The team then challenges the retreatants to do something with that knowledge: Spread the news that God is at the center of our desires, that love is the foundation of our lives, and that God brings new life to be shared. The dynamic is supported through a ritual commissioning within the Sunday Mass.

Time to Celebrate: Liturgy The Sunday morning Mass celebrates the retreatants' reconciliation and experience of God, the new friendships that have formed, and our role in spreading the Good News. Retreatants are invited to serve as ministers in the liturgy, filling such roles as lectors, altar servers, eucharistic ministers, greeters, musicians, and singers. (It is important that pastoral ministers prepare and train first-time liturgical ministers.) During the homily, they are invited to join with their small groups to name the charis—the grace, mercy, or gift—they received during the weekend. The eucharistic table becomes a table of gratitude for those gifts and a source of nourishment for the mission.

Because Charis retreats are geared toward young adults who may never have had parts of the Mass explained, a teaching Mass—in which the presider explains actions and prayers—can be helpful. Finally, after communion, a team member announces follow-up or ongoing young adult-ministry events, programs, and retreats sponsored by the host organization and its collaborators. Having a schedule of events or flyers at the entrance to the chapel is helpful. Participants are also asked to turn in evaluation forms as they leave the chapel or dining room.

Time to Say Good-bye Following Mass, all gather for a final meal together. This is often a time when people exchange contact information (though organizers can also provide information to all who request it and want it shared), analyze elements of the retreat, and even volunteer for future teams. While many are ready to go home, it is not unusual for some participants to linger for an hour or more after lunch, chatting with new friends, walking the grounds, or sitting silently in the chapel. The lunch and period afterward provide positive closure to the weekend.

Time to Evaluate After the good-byes, the team gathers to debrief. What was the grace for them as individuals and as a team? Where were the challenges or struggles? What worked logistically? What needs work for future retreats? Who might be invited to serve on future teams (based on behavior in small groups and on experiences on this retreat)? The written evaluations are reviewed, allowing immediate positive and constructive feedback for the dedicated volunteers.

Conclusion

Charis retreats welcome strangers to a life lived in and for Christ and others. Through reflection upon past experiences and naming where one has encountered God, sin, death, and reconciliation, we aim to lead the young adults into a lively relationship with the Holy and with the community of faith. &

CHAPTER 4

Selecting and Preparing the Team

The team members of a Charis retreat serve as the program's hospitality ministers, models of faith, and recruiters. With the guidance of pastoral staff, they plan and give the retreat, generously offering their own life experience, faith, time, energy, and love in the service of those who participate. Since the quality of the team and its preparation can make or break the retreat experience for participants and the credibility and relevance of the local program, it is one of the most important components of the Charis retreat.

The team experience in any retreat or pastoral program can be a powerful affirmation of belonging to the community of faith, both for the team and for those who benefit from the team's service. The team members may come to see their baptism in a new light. Their decision to serve on the team leads to a commitment to wrestle with the substance of their lives and to listen for the echoes of the Holy Spirit in their experiences. It prompts them to consider how they have lived and how they have experienced God. In poring over Scriptures to find ways in which their lives reflect the word, they find connections to the broader Christian community.

In linking life struggles to Catholic traditions—such as church documents, history, or the spirituality of saints—the team finds itself firmly held by generations of the Catholic community. We have seen conversions take place over the course of team preparation and retreat weekends. Young adults have moved from questioning seeker to still-questioning-but-impassioned evangelist of the Good News and of community membership and service.

Meeting team members who in some way reflect their own experiences can be the most powerful element of the retreat for participants. For a generation of people who have grown up in the wake of the "Me Generation," finding oneself to be like others and welcomed into an "us" community, even if only for a weekend, can be a transforming experience.

Many young adults come to retreats wondering if they are the only ones who pray and who consider God in making big decisions. Many come wondering if it is OK to question whether or not God exists, even while being a regular communicant.

> The more diverse the team, the more likely that every retreatant will feel comfortable with at least one member.

A diverse team that openly yet gently presents its life, faith, and questions tells the retreatants that they may do the same, that they belong in this community. Team selection is an effort to secure a variety of welcoming individuals who reflect the diverse young adult population in terms of their life experiences, demographics, vocations, personalities, and spiritualities, so that retreatants will feel understood and at ease.

Considerations in Choosing a Team

In considering who should be invited to serve on a Charis team, the experienced pastoral minister weighs a number of elements. If the goal of the retreat is to draw adults in their twenties and thirties into a deeper relationship with God in the context of the Catholic Christian tradition, it is helpful to know a variety of young adults who currently have such a relationship.

It is essential that the leader selecting the team pull from a pool of individuals who model the life of one actively looking for God in his or her life. Such leaders can be identified from past contacts (previous retreats or interactions in which the leader experienced their leadership and communications skills), other pastoral ministers, or the parents or peers of these faithful seekers. Most times, pastoral leaders or retreat directors will choose team members from previous retreatants because they are familiar with the retreat dynamic and because the leaders take comfort in knowing their personalities and faith journeys. From that pool, considerations in choosing the retreat team include the following.

Balance

A good team has a balance of genders, ages, vocations, spiritualities, ethnicities, marital status, and personalities. Too much similarity in these areas can lead to problems: Some retreatants won't be able to identify with the team, while others may have too much in common with team members. For example, an all-women team may lead to a heavily female retreat, and the few men who attend may feel out of place. Likewise, balancing the gender and age of team members guarantees a more representative group for the retreatants. The spectrum of vocations and professions is broad in the twenty- to forty-year-old age group, as are the spiritual practices. Therefore, the more diverse the team, the more likely that every retreatant will feel comfortable with at least one team member.

We have found that having a variety in the following areas works best:

- Gender diversity

- Age diversity. It is especially important to note that people in their early twenties may not identify with thirty-six- to forty-year olds and may not consider these individuals young adults. Balancing the team with one or two members in their early or mid-twenties, with the rest from twenty-five to thirty-five usually guarantees credibility and a young adult look. This also provides the option of reusing team members before they fall out of the age range.

- Ethnic diversity. Diverse team members have blessed the retreats by drawing young adults from their ethnic communities and by introducing people of other ethnicities to their traditions and experiences.

- Diversity of professions and vocations. People in their twenties and thirties occupy a wide range of professions and are often discerning whether their profession is their true calling. Therefore, having team members with a range of employment and vocational backgrounds helps retreatants feel welcome.

- Single and married people. We have found it helpful to have both married and single people on the team. Having at least one and possibly two married individuals allows those with the marriage vocation to give witness—and for some, hope—to young adults who are discerning that vocation. Similarly, having singles on the team affirms the graces that come with singleness as a transitory period of life or as a confirmed vocation.

- Diverse spiritualities. Many young adults are not familiar with traditional Catholic spiritualities. However, having at least one team member with some devotional practice or piety and at least one with some devotion to the Eucharist—especially in the Who Do You Say I Am? retreat and the Called and Chosen retreat—can serve to teach retreatants and welcome those with such devotions. It is also helpful to have at least one member who is familiar with non-Christian spiritualities, since many of the retreatants have been exposed to various spiritualities through friends, education, and popular culture.

- Diverse personalities. Try to have team members that among them possess the gifts of humor, serenity, gregariousness, warmth, honesty, and gentleness—and many more. This allows the retreatants to see how God moves in the variety of those gifts and in the variety of how people express those gifts through their interactions with others.

Life Experiences

Choosing a team with a diversity of life experiences adds to the richness of the retreat experience. In order to learn about their experiences, the pastoral minister must listen to the stories of potential team members: Where did they come from? What has led them to this point in their journey of life and faith? Who have been the important influences and relationships in their lives? Where have they found God? What have been the key experiences in their lives? Where have they felt broken or healed?

Listening to potential team members' responses can help the pastoral minister assess their maturity level and communication skills. It can also help the minister determine how well these candidates can relate their experiences to their faith. Listening can also help the minister balance the team. For example, if two or three people have had similar experiences that they would want to use for their talks, such as the sudden death of a parent, the minister can help the team members explore different aspects of that experience or even separate them into different retreat teams so that participants don't hear three very similar stories in one retreat.

It is important to listen graciously, even reverently, to the stories of retreatants.

Openness

It is essential that team members be able to share their experiences and to model the form of theological reflection that takes place in the retreat talks and small groups. When team members are comfortable and confident in speaking about personal experiences, display a degree of vulnerability, and name experiences, thoughts, and feelings while offering them to the Lord, retreatants feel empowered to do the same. The team members also need to be able to model appropriate boundaries when sharing and to be sensitive to the listeners. Openness should not be confused with the lack of boundaries. Retreatants come to be uplifted, not burdened with the graphic details of somebody's life.

Drawing Others Out

Team members who treat each person on the retreat as Christ or as an opportunity to experience grace are performing an act of service. As important as it is to model openness, it is equally important to listen graciously, even reverently, to the stories of retreatants. A team member who listens and who has the ability to gently affirm another allows retreatants to bring their lives before the community and the Lord safely at first and joyfully in the end.

Avoiding Overcommitments

It is frustrating to put together a wonderful team, only to find out that two members need to leave the retreat early, cannot make several of the prep meetings, or have finals the week before the retreat and are unprepared for the weekend. It is important that team members make time for their own preparation as well as time for the prep meetings, where they will form community among themselves, offer feedback, and receive valuable information and formation from the pastoral minister.

Summary

There is no ideal team when it comes to balance and diversity. Pastoral ministers should try to work toward balance and consider the areas noted above, but they should also realize that these are considerations, not qualifiers. Potential team members can be disqualified or not considered, however, if they would turn away retreatants because of their actions, if they have modeled inappropriate behaviors in previous interactions, or if they use their status as team members for their own personal or professional gain.

Inviting Team Members

We have found that the best way to invite young adults to become team members is through the early, direct, full-disclosure method. If five team members are needed, we identify ten individuals six to ten weeks before the retreat whom we would like to have on the team. Then we send e-mails to the first five individuals. (No mass e-mails for the invitations.) The e-mail contains

- an expressed interest in having the person serve on the retreat for a particular weekend;

- an outline of the time and energy commitment expected of the person if he or she accepts the invitation;

- a proposed schedule and summary of the team meetings;

- outlines of talks for him or her to review;

- a promise to follow up with a phone call to answer any questions or concerns;

- a deadline for him or her to respond; and

- a note of gratitude for considering the invitation.

Within a day or two of the e-mail, we follow up with a phone call to express interest, tell the individuals why we would like to have them on the team, and affirm the gifts we have observed in them. We tell them about the availability of a talk mentor, a pastoral minister who will be available to guide them, answer questions, and teach them before the retreat. We assure potential team members that they do not have to create the content of the retreat; they do not need to fear being on the team if it is their first time. The pastoral minister or talk mentor will be available for them before and/or during the retreat.

If the individuals are unavailable for the weekend of the retreat, unable to make the time commitment, are not ready to serve, or just say no, we thank them and ask if we may consider them for another retreat. We then invite another candidate who would lend balance to the team.

Forming Community Among Team Members

The preparation period leading up to the retreat can be like the team members' own retreat. It is important to emphasize that the preparation time spent together will benefit them as individuals and unify them as a group. The process of sharing talk ideas and life experiences, rehearsing talks, giving feedback, praying, and socializing together gives the team a head start in forming the retreat community.

For the individuals to develop into a team, several components should be built into the preparation. These include faith-sharing, prayer for one another and the retreatants, and an adequate number of meetings and sufficient lead time in advance of the retreat. Teams have formed outside the meetings in various ways—by choosing another member as a prayer partner, by reviewing each other's talks via e-mail, by keeping one another up to date on registrations, and by socializing after a meeting.

Team-Meeting Format

The team meetings follow a simple format. Because of busy schedules, evening or weekend meetings are easiest to attend. Meetings may be held at a parish meeting room, a team member's home, or elsewhere. We suggest the following format.

Dinner Especially if conducting an evening or an after-Mass meeting, dinner should be provided for the team to demonstrate care for their well-being and to help break the ice. Whether it's pizza, Chinese food, or fried chicken with side dishes, the team gets fueled up and grows closer around the table.

● ● ● ● ● ● ● ● ● ● ● ● ● ● ● ● ●

As with all the elements

of the retreat and its

preparation, we believe

in being systematic about

soliciting and providing

feedback for speakers.

● ●

Group Prayer This can be grace over the meal, but it should also include prayer as the meeting/training session begins and ends. The prayer should invoke the Holy Spirit's presence and the prayers of the patron saint of the parish or order. (We use St. Ignatius of Loyola, since the retreats are built on his Spiritual Exercises.) Prayer helps center the group and prepares them to approach their holy work. It brings closure to the meeting to offer prayers of gratitude, primarily for the service of the team, and petition. If the meeting takes place during a noteworthy feast day, month, or liturgical season, the pastoral minister may offer a ten-second catechesis on the subject.

Team Introductions Team members may or may not be familiar with one another, so a brief period should be set aside for formal introductions. Members may wish to share their parish affiliation (if applicable), something for which they are grateful that day, their favorite movie, or any other fact to help their new teammates get to know them.

Training This happens over several meetings. We devote at least part of a meeting, if not an entire three-hour block, to developing skills such as giving talks, facilitating small groups, and leading prayer. These areas are examined briefly in this chapter and more comprehensively in subsequent chapters.

As part of each area of training, we provide the following materials to assist the team:

- a binder for keeping materials together;

- team and retreatant schedules;

- talk development guidelines;

- outlines for various prayer services and tips for leading prayer; and

- handouts for small-group facilitation, including purpose, facilitator guidelines, and more.

Team-Training Meetings

We suggest having four or five meetings before the retreat. Most meetings will be around two hours plus dinner; none should be longer than three hours, including a fifteen-minute break. Several days before each meeting, an e-mail should be sent with the date, time, directions, and a reminder of the items to bring. Each e-mail should include a thank-you for the team's time and service.

Overview The first meeting is largely an introduction to the retreat topics, dynamics, and schedule. The schedule for future meetings (including a post-retreat team evaluation and reunion) is set. At this first meeting, we discuss in detail the schedule of retreat talks, and we ask team members for their first and second choices for talk topics. (Remember that the talk outlines were sent in advance of the first meeting.) The next two sets of meetings are devoted to the talks themselves.

Talks The purpose of the second meeting is to outline the talks. At this meeting, which happens at least three weeks before the retreat, each team member should present an outline with the following elements:

- a general overview of the talk he or she is presenting;

- the life or faith experiences that will be highlighted;

- Scripture that will be drawn upon or will frame the talk;

- songs he or she will use to introduce or close the talk; and

- questions that will be suggested for reflection.

The pastoral minister and team members give about thirty minutes of feedback to help focus the speaker's talk and to draw out the stories and Scriptures that will have the most impact on the audience.

The third meeting is actually a set of meetings. Often these are two meetings in the same week, at which team members are invited to both but are only required to attend one. The second of these meetings should take place no later than the Wednesday before the retreat; we suggest five to ten days prior to the retreat if possible.

At each of the two meetings, two or three team members run through their talks. The speakers take thirty-five minutes to rehearse their entire presentation, from the playing of the opening song to the presentation of reflection questions. Then they take three to ten days to fine-tune their talks before presenting them at the retreat. These two meetings are the longest preparation meetings. They may last as long as three hours so that the team members receive the best feedback.

Giving Feedback

As with all the elements of the retreat and its preparation, we believe in being systematic about soliciting and providing feedback for speakers. The format is intended to provide safety for the team member who is presenting and an opportunity for the other team members to practice their enthusiasm, gentleness, affirmation, care, and honesty. (See Chapter 5 for more on the objectives of the talks.)

> Visit **www.CharisRetreats.org** to download and customize talk materials.

We suggest the following strategies for giving feedback on the team members' talks and talk outlines.

Solicit Affirmation After presenters finish their talks or outlines, allow each of the other team members to name specific things that were effective, including structure and content. Speakers have been praised for including a particular life story, providing sensory details (such as what a key person smelled like when hugged), and using relevant Scripture. We have also heard compliments for introductions, transitions, pacing, and speaking in chronological order. As long as team members are honest, they cannot be too affirming during this segment. Pastoral ministers should model this feedback but should not necessarily go first. Instruct team members to avoid giving positive feedback that is dishonest, speaking in generalities when specifics can be identified, and taking more than five minutes per person.

Suggest Improvements Similar to the affirmations, the feedback should be specific about areas of improvement. Does the talk start strong but fade as it progresses? Has the speaker left out a reference to Scripture or tradition? Is it too graphic? Do too many stories or anecdotes cause listeners to lose the point? Is the person dispassionate or bored with his or her own presentation? Is the level of vulnerability or openness appropriate? Is the person's point consistent with the Good News?

Feedback should not include comments that judge the presenter's character or experience. While team members are welcome to question the level of sharing, it would be more harmful than constructive to tell someone who has shared a tender story that he or she is bad, crazy, or un-Christian. Sticking to questions such as "What was the Holy Spirit bringing about through this experience?" or "What in the story will serve our retreatants?" can help turn a judgmental comment into a constructive one.

Small-Group Facilitation Small-group facilitator training is key to the overall preparation of the team. At the retreat, team members are asked to facilitate (not lead or direct) members of a five to eight-person theological reflection and faith-sharing group. The role of the facilitator is to

- be yourself;
- model appropriate group behaviors and interactions (self-disclosure, active listening, responding);
- respect the confidentiality of all group members;
- keep the group on track;

> Do too many stories or anecdotes cause listeners to lose the point?

- stimulate discussion;

- protect the sense of belonging of each member and let each member be heard;

- allow quieter people opportunities to speak and more vocal individuals opportunities to listen;

- respect every person's right to choose not to speak;

- refrain from talking too much or monopolizing the group dynamic;

- allow for periods of silence;

- discourage generalizations from group members and ask them to use *I* and *me* instead of *you* and *we*;

- encourage members to speak about their own experiences instead of the experiences of others; and

- work for diffusion of leadership—gradually surrender the leadership role and embrace the role of group member.

Teams in Chicago and Cincinnati have conducted training for small-group facilitation as part of the pre-retreat team meetings for the talks and overview. In 2002–2003, the Chicago directors began conducting fall and spring training sessions on Saturday mornings for those wishing to serve on a Charis team in the coming months. This effort greatly expanded the pool of trained facilitators for Charis programs and small groups in local parishes. About thirty people attended each day, with three facilitators taking turns leading a three-hour program that included a continental breakfast and a coffee break. (See Chapter 7 for more on the purpose of small groups and other aspects of training.)

Small-Group Prayer Leadership Training

During the course of the meetings, either at the first meeting or at the meeting immediately prior to the start of the retreat, the pastoral ministers conduct the training for prayer leadership. (If a team member is leading an individual prayer service such as the Friday-night prayer, individual training is often given.) The group-prayer leadership training consists of demonstrating effective ways to lead healing prayer at the Saturday-evening service, roles and rehearsal for the Friday evening prayer, and other group-led prayers according to the particular Charis model that is being followed.

The Friday-Night Meeting

The team is asked to arrive at the retreat center as much as four hours before the retreat to check in, relax, help set up for the Friday-evening activities, and have a team meeting. The meeting is a time to commission the team members as servant-leaders, to be mindful of the presence of the Holy Spirit, and to pray for the team and the retreatants. The format consists of

- opening prayer;
- welcome for the team;
- run-through of the weekend's schedule, including time for questions and concerns;
- rehearsal of group prayer/skits for Friday night;
- reiteration of the role of the small-group facilitator and the group's guidelines;
- last-minute instructions for the evening;
- a giant thank-you for the team's time, energy, and service thus far; and
- prayer for the person who will be giving the talk that night.

Meetings During the Retreat

It is crucial to have several brief and some longer team meetings during the retreat weekend itself. These meetings allow for feedback for speakers, prayers of thanksgiving and petition (especially for the Spirit to lead the next speaker), the opportunity to raise questions and concerns about small groups or individuals, reiteration of the schedule, and opportunity to check in with and thank team members for their time and energy.

Evaluation/Reunion Meetings

At the end of the retreat, after the packing is done and the retreatants have gone home, it is important for the team to debrief. An hour is set aside to ask "What were the blessings?" and "What could be improved?"

The evaluation forms from the retreatants are reviewed, and the team notes the names of those who volunteered to serve on future teams. Small-group facilitators are asked to give recommendations about the readiness of those in their small groups who volunteered to be future facilitators. The team members are thanked again and sent on their way.

A reunion/post-retreat-evaluation dinner is usually held two to three weeks after the retreat. This allows the team to continue to process what happened on the retreat and to offer constructive feedback on the format, talk content, and possible team members. It also allows the group, who by now have bonded through their shared service, to relax, socialize, and be grateful together.

Conclusion

The team for a Charis program is one of the most valuable components of the retreat. Pastoral ministers should take the time to carefully select diverse members who compose a balanced group. Skillful and loving preparation provides the team with the tools necessary to be servant-leaders. The preparation period also allows the team members an extended retreat experience. Finally, a well-prepared team blesses the retreatants with models of hospitality and generosity who can articulate their faith and their struggles. ⚜

A well-prepared team blesses the retreatants with models of hospitality and generosity who can articulate their faith and their struggles.

CHAPTER **5**

Sharing the Story: Developing and Giving Retreat Talks

From the beginning of our Judeo-Christian tradition, stories have served as a primary means of preserving and passing on the faith. The sacred texts of the Hebrew and Christian Scriptures are stories of the relationship of God with God's beloved people. We retell these stories each time we gather in Catholic worship.

Stories are also important in the tradition of Ignatian spirituality. The spirituality of the Incarnation rests upon this central theme: When the Word became flesh and dwelt among us in the Person of Jesus, the lived stories of all people and all creation were made holy. No person, no experience, no emotion, and no concern are beyond God's loving reach. As the poet Gerard Manley Hopkins said, "The world is charged with the grandeur of God."[1] St. Ignatius of Loyola therefore invites his followers to find God in all things.

For many people today, including many young adults, the idea that God could be present in *all* things is unimaginable. Surely, God is found only in the best of times, the greatest of achievements, the proudest of moments. With this operating principle, we bring to light only what our culture rewards as brightest in our lives, carefully keeping the rest of life in the shadows. Meanwhile, important parts of our story remain hidden, leaving us to suffer our secrets alone. One retreat master on a Charis retreat attempted to illuminate the darkness in a sermon by asking his young adult congregation, "If Jesus showed up to visit you tonight, what would you most hope he wouldn't bring up?"

One of the main goals of Charis retreats is to enable young adults to bring into Christ's light the full range of their stories and experiences. This allows them to realize where God is most active in their lives, which may be in unlikely places.

Personal stories of faith, therefore, form the backbone of Charis young adult retreats. Stories are told through four or five faith-sharing talks given at intervals throughout the retreat. The talks offer both inspirational content and a model that shows retreatants how to reflect on their own stories and how to share their life experiences in small groups or one-on-one sessions.

A Charis faith-sharing talk comprises four elements. First, the bulk of the talk draws from the speaker's own experiences, his or her "life stuff." Second, the talk weaves in and illuminates elements of Scripture and our rich faith tradition—the lives of holy men and women, sacraments, or significant prayers and beliefs. Third, the talk begins and ends with a work of art—usually a song, but sometimes a brief video, poem, photo, or painting—that underscores the talk's central message. Fourth, the talk leads naturally to a few printed reflection questions that invite the retreatants to mine for the gold in their own life experiences. The talk, including its artistic elements, typically lasts thirty minutes and leads into at least thirty minutes of individual reflection time with the questions.

> Paint pictures with words to create dramatic scenes as if the audience were watching a movie.

Each talk serves as the centerpiece for a particular movement of the Charis retreat. In the first movement on Friday night, for example, the speaker offers an overview of his or her life story, focusing on significant moments. This talk fits within the beginning movement of the retreat, which introduces retreatants to the concepts of looking for the workings of God in significant life events and beginning to share those events with one another. The first speaker should, therefore, tell a story that shows him or her to be somewhat vulnerable, but the talk should not be so deeply confessional that it reveals too much intimacy or heaviness before the retreatants have settled in.

Later, on Saturday evening, the talk sets the stage for considering suffering, healing, and hope, and leads into a reconciliation service. At this point, after several sessions of small-group sharing and several reflection periods, retreatants are ready for the greatest level of intimacy with God and with one another, so the speaker can appropriately share more intimate stories. By

Most young adult team members are insightful in sharing their own experiences.

Sunday morning, the talk leads into the movement from the retreat back to daily life, and so the subject matter of the talk should not be heavy or sorrowful. Instead, it should be focused on leading and missioning people to take the retreat out into the world.

Because the talks are so central to Charis retreats, a great deal of training and resources are devoted to developing them. Each young adult speaker is assigned a talk mentor, a person with pastoral ministry training and familiarity with Charis. The main role of the mentor is to assist the speaker in weaving elements from our faith tradition into the talk. In our experience, most young adult team members are articulate and insightful in sharing their own experiences, but they need help choosing and incorporating related elements of our faith tradition (Scripture, sacraments, and so on). At the same time, retreatants are hungry for solid faith-based content; while they might enjoy a good story, they have expressed disappointment when it does not further their growth in knowledge of the faith. Talk mentoring ensures the inclusion and soundness of theological content, and many speakers have benefited personally from these meetings as a type of spiritual direction for the speakers, themselves.

In addition to talk mentoring, each speaker has an opportunity to practice the talk with other team members before giving it on the retreat. During practice, the talks are timed. Other team members assist the speaker in determining "where the gold is" in the talk. They give feedback on what parts are the most engaging and what improvements can be made.

Twelve Suggestions for Effective Faith-Sharing Talks

The following suggestions can aid speakers in developing and evaluating their talks.

1. Choose Stories the Audience Can Relate To

In determining what stories are relatable, consider the life experiences of the audience as well as the developmental tasks of young adulthood. Most young adults are searching for a life partner or a welcoming community, desiring intimacy in relationships, trying to build competence in meaningful study or work, and seeking to establish a new identity in relation to their families of origin, in-laws, and schoolmates. Stories succeed when they touch on these and other young adult themes. On the other hand, stories about grandchildren or retirement would probably not connect with the average young adult. Similarly, less universal experiences such as formation in a monastery or the birth of a child will not be as accessible for an audience of mostly laypeople without children.

2. Choose Stories That Reach an Appropriate Level of Intimacy

As mentioned before, it is important that the retreat talks show who the speakers are beneath the surface, with some level of vulnerability and a humanness that connects deeply with the audience. This enables retreatants to be more open before God and one another. The challenge comes in knowing how deep to go and what subject matter to share. While there is no set rule, the following questions might serve as guides: Am I able to talk about this without reducing myself or my audience to a sobbing mess? What benefits might come from this story? A traumatic event that happened last week might be too raw to point anywhere beyond the pain of the experience, while one that has been worked through over time and distance might offer rich wisdom.

3. Have a Clear Theme and Purpose

In planning a talk, always start with the purpose or theme—the main points the experience illustrates—and work backward from there. A story can be relatable and interesting, but its value is limited if it does not point somewhere larger.

The resource book for each retreat provides sample reflection questions for each talk.

Visit www.CharisRetreats.org to download and customize reflection questions.

It is up to the retreat coordinator to decide which questions to use. A practical way to get started is to spend time with the reflection questions for the talk. The questions are designed to open up one's life experience and to stimulate reflection and small-group sharing. For a talk on relationships, for example, the following might be useful:

- Describe two or three relationships in your life that have helped shape the person you are.

- How have you experienced change within a relationship?

- Which relationships are strong for you right now? Do any need special attention or work?

Use these questions as a guide to review the experiences that might shape your talk. Then once the talk is developed, check back with the questions to make sure your talk is responsive to one or more of them.

One consideration in developing talks is that the retreat is moving toward the celebration of Sunday's liturgy with the whole church around the world. In light of that, incorporating some of the themes or images from Sunday's readings can lead retreatants into an especially powerful experience of some of the gifts of Catholicism: universality, interconnectedness between liturgy and life, and the relationship of ancient Scripture to contemporary experience. It would be ideal to build into your talk or prayer a theme or an image that relates to the readings. But it isn't a problem if Sunday's Scriptures don't fit your talk.

4. Connect with the Audience

At the beginning of the story, identify the experience as one shared by and relevant to the audience. This need not be elaborate and will normally happen naturally, but it must be included. The opening should attempt to tie in the talk with what has occurred thus far on the retreat or with the retreat as a whole. The talk should close with a transition into the next segment. For example, if the next segment is reflection or small-group time, one approach is to turn the question to the audience: "This is my experience of suffering, healing, and hope—what about you? What in your own life may have similarly changed you? To help you reflect on this, we are passing out some questions."

5. Show as Much as Tell

Paint pictures with words to create dramatic scenes as if the audience were watching a movie. Use details such as "My father filled up the whole doorway," "that dentist's-office smell," "her heels clacking fast and loud on the tile floor."

6. Use Narrative, Fast-Forward, or Slices of Life

For stories with a distinct beginning, middle, and end, the best way to tell them is usually as a chronological narrative: what happened next, and after that, and after that. Often, however, the lessons of life come to us as more of a three-dimensional collage than a neat, linear progression. Meanings may only be clear after the lapse of many years or after a composite of various experiences. To avoid the trap of trying to bridge a five-year gap in the story with irrelevant details from the intervening time, some speakers say "Fast-forward five years. Once again I am sitting on my grandmother's porch." Or offer the talk as a series of scenes, or slices of life, with clean breaks and a pause between each.

7. Choose a Fitting Tone

The tone of the story should fit the lesson being taught and create the attitude for what follows the talk. The tone of the talk that is the introduction to the retreat should be welcoming and hopeful for all that lies ahead on the retreat. By contrast, the tone of the "Suffering, Healing, and Hope" talk leading into Saturday night's reconciliation service should be more solemn, though it may contain moments of comic relief.

8. Use Tone of Voice and Body Language

If a moment in the story is sad, use a serious look and tone of voice, perhaps whispering a few words. For anger, raise the volume. At key moments or turning points, consider pausing and silently counting to four to let the experience sink in.

9. Identify the Feeling Level of the Story

Good stories touch the heart, not just the head. Feelings can be named directly: "I was so hurt." "I felt angry." "I was overjoyed." Feelings can also be shown: "Tears filled his eyes." "I put my face in my hands." Let the tone of voice and expression also convey that feeling.

10. Use Religious Language

Let's face it: There are few work or social settings where it is considered cool to talk directly and personally about God, Jesus, or one's prayer experience. One of the goals of a retreat, however, is to create a space in which it is safe to speak intimately of one's life of faith—whether it be a place of struggle and search or richness and nourishment. In giving talks, therefore, try to build up a comfort level with using religious language. This doesn't mean becoming a televangelist shouting a barrage of pious verbiage at people. Instead, talk straightforwardly about an experience of the sacred. Think over the names for the Holy One that draw you in and use them naturally in the talk: God, Jesus, Spirit, Source of Life, Friend. This frees retreatants to give voice to their own faith and experience of God.

> One of the great hungers of young adults is for knowledge of our faith tradition, since many are deprived of it.

11. Link the Story with Our Faith Tradition

One of the great hungers of young adults is for knowledge of our faith tradition, since many are unfamiliar with it. Retreatants benefit from the richness of a speaker's experience, but they are not truly nourished by a talk unless it provides them with content they can use again. There may be a Scripture passage that fits naturally with the talk, such as the story of the prodigal son. Maybe a story offers an everyday experience of the Beatitudes, the Corporal Works of Mercy, or the Eucharist. Or there might be a saint whose life a story recalls. These connections can be woven throughout the talk or introduced at the beginning or the end.

12. Practice! Practice! Practice!

Usually if a story doesn't go well, it simply needs better telling. Perhaps the story needs a clear, concise ending to bring it in for a landing. Some parts might need to be rearranged or omitted to tighten up the story. Timing the story and cutting nonessential parts might also help.

Conclusion

Whatever else we have said about the faith-sharing talks can be boiled down to this: They are much more than simply talks. A talk is not meant to be an end in itself, a therapeutic experience for the speaker, or a chance to hear the sound of one's own voice. Instead, a person who stands before others and opens up his or her life and faith is giving a generous gift to listeners—the gift of the speaker's unique glimpse of the face of God.

Talks on Charis retreats, therefore, are a way of listening for the retreatants who hear them. They are designed to tap into the events, themes, and feelings in the listeners' own experiences. Talks prime the pump that enables retreatants to drink deeply from their own sacred wells—and later to share some of that living water with others in small groups, prayer, and liturgy. ⚘

CHAPTER 6

Starting the Retreat: Christian Hospitality and Welcome

Two of the most important elements in young adult ministry are the invitation and the welcome. With that in mind, this chapter will address how to welcome retreatants from the time they inquire about the program to the end of the first block of presentation, reflection, small-group time, and prayer. It will further address how to invite participants into the retreat atmosphere and how to balance invitation with respect for individual needs.

Grounding and Theology of Retreat Hospitality

Our model for retreat hospitality flows from the Gospels. In the stories of Jesus and his friends Mary, Martha, and Lazarus, we see that the house in Bethany was one of hospitality for and encounter with the Lord. Martha scurries about to tidy the house, set the table, and prepare the meal. We imagine a flurry of activity to make the house presentable and comfortable before Jesus arrives.

Yet Martha also prepares a space where she and her sister, Mary, may encounter not just any guest, but *the* guest, their Lord. Mary is free, thanks to her sister's preparations (and likely her own, before Jesus' arrival), to sit at the feet of the Lord, to listen, to be taught, and to be loved. Even later in the Gospel when Jesus comes to Bethany, the sisters—their hearts full of grief and reproach, but also gratitude and faith—clear a space for Jesus to mourn and then to do the work of raising their brother, Lazarus, from the dead.

Elsewhere in the Gospels, in Jesus' calling of the Twelve, we have a model for direct invitation to those we meet and to those in need of the Good News. In Jesus' eating with sinners and his willingness to draw followers from among the unpopular or scandalous, we see that all are welcome at his table. In his journeying to celebrate a wedding, to have a well-prepared meal, and to mourn with friends, we see Jesus longing to be with us in both joy and pain. And in his encounter with the Samaritan woman, we are made aware that he knows our stories, our desires, and our sins. We know that he loves us wholeheartedly and that he wants to save us, regardless of our shortcomings.

It follows, then, that the Charis team's actions of invitation and welcome are grounded in Jesus' own ministry and in the Gospel stories of those who prepared a place for Jesus. The way we conduct ourselves shows the retreatant who we are and what we are about. This begins with welcoming language in publicity materials and continues with warm, friendly contact each time an organizer or a volunteer engages a potential retreatant. As Christians, we prepare a space as the sisters in Bethany did—with competence, consideration, and the goal of preparing the way for Jesus to do his work. We invite others—as Jesus did—with warmth, directness, confidence, and a genuine desire to spend time with them. We demonstrate the message of the Charis retreats: God wants to be with us, to grace us, to share in our joy and pain, to heal us, to comfort us, to bring us our heart's desire, and to save us.

Pre-Retreat Hospitality

Each time a young adult calls, e-mails, or approaches a volunteer to inquire about a Charis program, we have an opportunity to model Christian hospitality. A potential retreatant's questions about format, content, and logistics should be answered with competence and genuine enthusiasm. All publicity and follow-up information should convey that participants are welcome to attend regardless of their life experience. The organizers should make clear that they are excited that the person is considering attending. They should also express that the team will pray for the person as he or she prepares for the retreat.

When the retreatant registers in advance of the retreat, the registrar should offer sincere words of welcome. Being direct and friendly in all communication can help the potential participant feel less like an outsider and more like a member of a community. Therefore, organizers should take great pains to provide clear and concise travel directions, payment options, lists of what to bring, and a general overview for the weekend. Questions should be answered as competently and as completely as possible, either by the registrar or by the pastoral minister or team members. To accommodate retreatants' physical needs during the weekend, they should be asked if they have dietary restrictions, impaired mobility, or other special considerations.

At the retreat itself, team members or other volunteers greet each participant at the entrance. A warm smile from volunteers puts newcomers at ease, and an organized registration instills confidence that the retreat is worthwhile and that the retreatants' time, effort, and decision to attend are appreciated. Each retreatant is welcomed with the following items:

- schedule
- name tag
- map of the facility (could be placed in person's room)
- house rules (could be placed in person's room)
- emergency-contact form
- other necessary materials

The team member accepts final payment if the retreatant has not already paid in full. Retreatants are then invited to dinner if provided or to the welcome session and (if on a weekend retreat) shown to their private rooms to settle in. (We recommend that each retreatant have his or her own private room to facilitate rest, prayer, individual silent reflection, and a break from the group dynamic.)

Whether or not to begin the retreat with a meal depends on considerations such as cost, furnishings, and the ability of the team and retreatants to arrive at the retreat center in time for an evening meal.

Team and Retreatant Introductions

Hospitality continues with introductions over dinner or in the first session. If dinner is provided, the team and participants may introduce themselves over dessert. We recommend a simple introduction: name, parish (if applicable), school or city affiliation, interesting fact. The team should go first to model the type of introduction the retreatants should give. For less formal introductions, the team might schedule an icebreaker prior to the official start of the retreat. The goal of this type of introduction is for the team and the participants to learn a few names, get a sense of what the group is like, and set a level of psychological comfort.

 See Chapter 6 of the retreat resource books for more on icebreakers.

Opening Session

After dinner but before the first talk and small-group gathering, the entire group gathers in a conference room or chapel to listen to a presentation by the team. The presentation serves to provide a foundation for the retreat by

- welcoming retreatants again;
- introducing prayer as a central component;
- suggesting why one might make a retreat;
- explaining the philosophy and theology underlying a Charis retreat;
- outlining the format and elements of the retreat;
- introducing guidelines and expectations for participants;
- providing an overview of the logistics of the facility;
- referring to activities on the schedule; and
- explaining the guidelines for small-group participation.

Opening Prayer

For each of the Charis Seekers' Retreats, the formal program opens with a prayer and a video presentation. The opening prayer may be as simple as lighting a large candle while reading a Scripture passage. In the Chicago and Cincinnati Seekers' Retreats, we have used the passage "[S]eek and you will find; knock and the door will be opened to you." (Matthew 7:7) This Scripture may be proclaimed or performed as a skit by the team.

A transition is made to a music video that portrays images of the experiences of young adults and captures the retreat theme. The video is shown, and then the pastoral minister or director ties together the reading and the video, offering an opening blessing for the retreat. The large candle is usually referred to as a Christ candle. It is lit whenever the entire group is gathered for a presentation or communal prayer.

Retreat Overview

Following the opening prayer and video presentation, the team members present elements of the retreat overview. The purpose of this presentation is to put the group at ease and to alleviate some of their fears. The team encourages openness and discusses how a retreat can be of value. This presentation sets norms for appropriate behavior that can be unique to a retreat. It also suggests how we can get to know one another while allowing the participants to gain a better understanding of themselves and their relationship with the divine. It is helpful to provide in advance all the information discussed below, either through e-mail or direct mail before the retreat, or as a handout as the retreatants register. The overview may include the following elements.

Reasons to Come on Retreat

The following points should be addressed by the team members. (Detailed talking points are covered in the retreat resource books.)

- A retreat is time away.

- What a retreat is not

- People come to retreats for a variety of reasons.

Unique Characteristics of a Charis Retreat

Charis is from the Greek, meaning "grace," "mercy," or "manifestation of the divine." We recognize that God works in our lives constantly. God continually gives us gifts of mercy, healing, companionship, and God's own presence. We use the word *charis* to describe those gifts, that grace of the Holy Spirit, that movement of God in our innermost heart and in our everyday lives. We come to a Charis retreat to look for moments of charis, to ask for more spiritual gifts, and to celebrate God's ongoing presence in our lives. Address the unique format of a Charis retreat and discuss its special relevance to young adults.

Format of a Charis Retreat

A Charis retreat consists of five blocks. Following is a brief overview of the elements that make up the blocks. (Chapter 3 includes detailed information on each block.)

Presentation by a young adult Presentations are heavily autobiographical and are based in Scripture.

Silent reflection time Speakers conclude their talks with questions for reflection. Individual reflection time follows.

Small groups All have the opportunity to gather in peer-facilitated small groups to safely share their reflections.

Prayer and conferences with spiritual director During individual reflection time, retreatants may choose to meet one-on-one with a trained spiritual director to discuss their reflections, experiences, or faith journey.

Communal Prayer on a Charis Retreat

At various points throughout the retreat, participants have opportunities for formal, shared prayer. This includes the Catholic Mass and a communal reconciliation service. It also includes the introduction of various prayer forms in the mornings and evenings, such as guided meditation, Ignatian contemplation, the *examen*, movement prayer, and other prayers that the team considers appropriate.

Silence as a Key Element

Silence is an important element of the retreat. In the busy world of a young adult—with responsibilities to work, friends, and family—a retreat is a time apart, a time when he or she can be silent. It is essential on the first night to stress the importance of silence. (Chapter 8 includes more detail on sacred silence.)

Guidelines for Retreat Etiquette

Establishing team and participant guidelines and expectations for behavior is a primary part of the retreat overview. In a generation in which sex, crime, and personal scandals are freely discussed, God and religion have become the topics most forbidden. It is the area most intimate and therefore most difficult to reveal or share with peers.

During the retreat, we want participants to feel safe to pray and to express their feelings and thoughts about their relationship to God. We hope that they may be able to "sit at the feet of the Lord" by listening to their own and others' experience of Jesus. Therefore, we set specific guidelines regarding confidentiality, appropriate sharing, and social behaviors.

> During the retreat, we want participants to feel safe to pray and to express their feelings and thoughts about their relationship to God.

For example, we note that while the social component may be appealing, participants should not feel they have the right to interrupt another's silence during reflection, meals, or other unstructured time. There should not be a club atmosphere, and the exchange of personal contact information should be reserved for the end of the retreat. We know of at least four happy marriages that have come out of Cincinnati and Chicago retreat weekends. The pastoral ministers in attendance can confirm that those relationships did not begin with someone putting the moves on another during the retreat.

Similarly, business pitches should wait until retreat reunions, if then. Retreatants do not spend time discerning whether to come to a spiritual weekend so that they can be greeted by commercials for photographers or time-share opportunities. Retreat etiquette demands that participants honor one another's time with God away from the business and consumer world.

We are also aware that participants come with varying degrees of involvement and piety and that they bring different prayer experiences. We ask that participants respect one another's level of involvement and not judge, attempt to proselytize, or debate while on the retreat. The weekend is a time to be open to what God has in store for you, not what you think God is planning for your neighbor. The retreat is a safe place where we may feel God's love for us, not judgment from our neighbor. It is a place where the retreatant may feel the hospitality of others, hear the invitation of Jesus, and be able to respond to it safely.

House Logistics

If rules and logistics are not provided before the retreat or upon check-in, a team member or the retreat center's coordinator could remind participants of house logistics, including the locations of bathrooms, smoking areas, first-aid supplies, snacks, and phones (for emergencies).

In addition, it's helpful to review the layout of the grounds; discuss the rules for the chapel, such as no eating; request the emergency-contact information if not already collected; and reiterate any other house rules. A map and a written list of the above information should be left in each retreatant's room prior to the retreat. If there are other groups in the facility, retreatants should be reminded to respect their silence and space.

Small-Group Overview

Finally, the guidelines for small-group sharing are outlined to retreatants. Elements of this outline include reasons for having small groups, the guidelines, and the arrangement of the groups. (See Chapter 7 for more on small groups.)

Icebreaker

If an icebreaker event has not already been held, the start of the retreat is a good time to take a break, get people moving, and provide an opportunity to mingle before the first presentation, reflection, and small-group block.

Friday Dinner

Cost is an important consideration in planning the Friday dinner. Since retreat houses charge by room and by meals, a single meal for retreatants can add a significant expense to the cost of the retreat.

In Chicago, retreats typically begin with a table ministry of pizza, usually ordered in because the center's dinner time is earlier than the retreat's scheduled dinner. The dinner is a wonderful way for people to unwind and to meet, and ordering out is usually less expensive than paying for the retreat center's evening meal. The drawback is that if dinner runs long, it may delay the beginning of the opening session and cause the entire evening to run late.

In Cincinnati, retreats begin with a reception of heavy hors d'oeuvres— enough for a meal if retreatants did not have dinner, but light enough that those who already ate can nibble. The reception is held in the same room as the opening session so that the food draws people in.

A less expensive option is to choose a facility where the team and retreatants can cook their own meals. This requires more planning, but it can lead to more bonding. In whatever way your team decides to handle meals, nothing says welcome like food with new friends after a long week.

Conclusion

A retreatant experiences welcome both before and during a Charis retreat. We follow the example of Jesus and his friends by warmly inviting, by accommodating group and individual needs, and by creating a space where each retreatant may directly encounter the Lord. ⚭

CHAPTER 7

Creating and Tending Small Groups

Overview: Small Groups on Charis Retreats

This chapter is designed to offer a broad overview of the nature of Charis small groups. It provides guidelines for retreat-group functioning and a description of the life cycle of the small group throughout the weekend. To get an idea of the purpose of small groups on Charis retreats, it helps to note that they are rooted in Scripture.

One significant Scripture passage is the story of the road to Emmaus. (Luke 24:13–35) This Gospel story tells of two disciples who are walking along the road together, dejected after the crucifixion of their friend and teacher. Then a stranger joins them and asks what they are talking about. The stranger remains anonymous and, instead of explaining to them that Jesus has risen, poses a question that guides the disciples deeper into their story. The two travelers are so enlivened and consoled by the conversation that they invite the stranger to stay with them that evening. Later, after Scripture and bread are broken open, the two recognize the stranger in their midst as none other than their friend and teacher, Jesus. They report Christ's presence among them to the wider community, recalling how their hearts were burning as they walked and talked with him on the road.

In Charis small groups, we relive the Emmaus story in a sense. Those who are traveling this road of contemporary life come together, usually as strangers. Like Jesus, the group leader does not explain or lecture but may pose a question or two designed to take retreatants deeper into their own stories. The small group becomes a place where a wide array of life experiences, emotions, and faith can be shared.

With openness, encouragement, and compassion, small groups can empower each member to find his or her own authentic voice. Some may find themselves telling of experiences or sharing vulnerability never before expressed to anyone. Some may find common ground and learn that they are not the only ones who struggle with sexuality, who wonder whether God cares or even exists, or who are contemplating a change of direction in their lives. Many encounter the sacred space where God is incarnate in all parts of life—"God in all things," as St. Ignatius put it. And often, small groups are a place where hearts are burning.

> With openness, encouragement, and compassion, small groups can empower each member to find his or her own authentic voice.

For these reasons, one of the most important components of Charis retreats is the small group. Each of these gatherings follows the reflection period after each retreat talk. Ideally, small groups consist of five to eight participants, as well as a team member who serves as facilitator. Groups meet five or six times over the course of the weekend to enable retreatants to share experiences, hopes, dreams, fears, triumphs, failures, life, and prayer in a safe and intimate setting. Through compassionate listening and encouragement, small groups help each member see himself or herself through God's loving and affirming eyes.

Charis small groups offer benefits and gifts such as healing, transformation, intimate connection, and community. At the same time, a negative small-group experience on a retreat has much potential to do damage. Therefore, a great deal of effort is put into training team members in facilitating small groups and also in setting norms with retreatants for optimal small-group interaction.

Although retreatants often arrive as persons unknown to the team, some effort is also made to arrange the small groups with care. For example, we have found it best to separate spouses, boyfriends and girlfriends, roommates, and those who ask us to keep them separate. We have found it beneficial to pay attention to such categories as gender and ethnicity. We also try to avoid having someone feel isolated or in need of "translation" because he or she is the only man, woman, or person of color in a group. Although groups can work without taking these steps, these practices create added safety and security for retreatants.

Additionally, benefits can come from arranging small groups by gender or age. Retreatants can benefit from being arranged into small groups for those in their early twenties and others for those thirty and over. Likewise, retreatants have sometimes found enhanced support from being in all-male or all-female small groups. If the circumstances and numbers make it feasible, single-sex small groups could be offered, perhaps as one option among others.

Depth of Charis Small Groups

Now let us define the purpose of the Charis small group. First of all, the group is limited by time; it will only meet over the course of the retreat. A day- or weekend-long group is the most that can be assumed. Therefore, although some may find participation in the group therapeutic and healing, all should be mindful that this is not a therapy group or even a small community of long-term duration. Moreover, the facilitator is a team member, not a trained psychotherapist. His or her role is to share life experiences with the group and to help others hear the voice of the Spirit in the gathered community.

For these reasons, every effort should be made to keep the conversation at an appropriate level, without self-disclosure of a type that becomes too threatening to the person or to the group as a whole. Thus, retreatants should not be urged to encounter current relationships within the group, such as confronting other group members with animosity or challenge. Similarly, retreatants should not be pushed to disclose too much information, such as discussing highly personal problems and situations usually reserved for a relationship with a psychotherapist. Examples of threatening self-disclosure might include dwelling on one's inclination to commit suicide or giving extended and graphic detail about sexual practices. Though struggles and concerns about suicide, depression, and sexuality are certainly topics that arise in small groups, the threat level is based more on the degree or depth of sharing ("How fresh is this wound?" for example) rather than on the subject area itself. Furthermore, for matters that might be too personal for the small-group setting, retreatants have the opportunity for one-on-one spiritual direction, pastoral counseling, and sacramental reconciliation.

Notwithstanding the best of training and intentions, sometimes groups or their members can wander into areas they are not equipped to handle. A technique for remedying such a situation is the Pause Rule. If a person in the group feels that he or she has already shared too much and too personally or does not want to share anymore, he or she can simply raise a hand in a "stop" gesture. The conversation should then be steered to another topic, or the leader or another speaker may begin talking. Also, if any group member feels that the speaker or group member has become uncomfortably intense or that the conversation is too difficult for him or her to handle, that member or the leader may use the same gesture. Handled with sensitivity and understanding, this technique has served as an effective way to switch gears and maintain a healthy group interaction.

Too much depth on the retreat is not desirable, and neither is superficiality. Three or four sessions in a retreat are usually enough to move the group beyond small talk, icebreakers, generalizations, thoughts, and ideas. Many find it helpful to share personal experiences from the past, as well as current problems, issues, and situations. They can especially benefit from speaking with genuineness and feeling. For these reasons, we encourage people to use the word *I* to tell their stories rather than generalizing. They should also speak from their own experience rather than from someone else's.

See the retreat resource books for training handouts about groups and the Pause Rule. (Visit www.CharisRetreats.org to download and customize these handouts.)

Finally, special power can emerge when one's personal story or life experience is joined with our faith tradition. Jesus did this in the Emmaus story when he linked the disciples' experience with all of Scripture. So too, group leaders and members can enrich one another's stories by pointing to connections with Scripture, the saints, and other elements of our Christian story.

Time Considerations

Charis small groups are limited not only by the event's duration, but also by the specific time blocks they occupy within a tightly scheduled retreat. No one is afforded the luxury to share what, for example, a forty-eight-consecutive-hour encounter group might offer. To realize the benefits of all the retreat's components and to respect the need for such things as rest, recreation, and contemplative time, it is essential to keep to the schedule and to honor the time allotted for each small-group session.

Leaders and group members must pay attention to how much time is available for each session and must ensure that each person has an opportunity to speak. In Charis, the norm is that each person must have an initial opportunity to speak before others may speak for a second time. Once all have had an opportunity to share if they so desire, the ideal small group will move into free-flowing conversation, which may be punctuated by periods of quiet. In the course of that conversation, the small-group leader continues to tend the group by drawing out the quieter members and keeping the group on topic. Throughout the meeting, the small-group leader attends to the time.

Other Group Norms

In addition to considerations about time and depth of sharing, several other important norms contribute to the safety and effectiveness of small groups during the retreat. Leaders announce these norms to all the retreatants at the start of the retreat and again at the start of the first small-group session.

Confidentiality

Everything shared within the small group stays within the small group. Confidentiality counteracts the inhibiting fear that someone's self-revelation might become fodder for gossip or might cause other damage. Confidentiality not only prohibits group members from disclosing to outsiders what is shared in the group, but it also prohibits group members from discussing someone's sharing among themselves in that person's absence. Each person's words and experiences are respected, treated as holy, and held within the safe container of the small community to whom they are offered.

Passing

Of course, retreatants are invited and encouraged to take an active role in small-group conversation. Anyone's witness to his or her own life experience is a sacred and generous act for others in the group. Nonetheless, there are times when one is not yet ready to speak, when an experience or struggle or question is too painful to share, or when speaking might leave one too vulnerable. Accordingly, a retreatant who feels he or she is not ready to share may simply say "Pass." That person may or may not feel safer taking a turn later in the session or in another session.

No-J.A.B. Rule

This rule prohibits group members from responding to someone's sharing by Judging, Advice-giving, or Blaming. The value of small groups is that they enable members to express their experiences, emotions, and faith. Members need to be allowed to experience, hear, and understand the small community. The No-J.A.B. Rule encourages redemptive listening by forbidding behaviors that silence others.

Judging and blaming can damage someone who has made himself or herself vulnerable in front of the group. Judging comes across in statements such as "It sounds like you don't pray enough . . . If you were a better husband, then . . . That was a stupid thing to do . . ." Blaming may be expressed in comments such as "That was your own fault . . . That would never have happened if you hadn't . . ." Most of us already experience advertising, societal values, and our own internal critics working overtime to remind us of the ways we are not good enough and have failed.

In contrast, a Charis small group should offer a chance to see ourselves as God sees us—with love, care, and compassion. Group members can help one another by showing with their eyes, facial expressions, and postures that they are listening. They can relay understanding, paraphrase what the person has said, name the feelings that might lurk beneath the experience, or ask questions that lead deeper into the matter. "That must have been really scary when your sister was diagnosed . . . Did anything especially help you get through that time? . . . I'm really struck by how much you were able to rely on other people's prayers . . ."

The value of small groups is that they enable members to express their experiences, emotions, and faith.

It is also appropriate to have a no "cross-talk" rule. This allows a person's words to land in the holy silence that follows sharing, instead of having other group members immediately react to what was shared or insert their own experiences. The listeners' goal is to respond with expressions or words that are genuine, compassionate, and encouraging.

Advice-giving takes the form of group members telling the person sharing how he or she should solve a problem. While this might be appropriate in a Dear Abby column or a law office, it can be destructive in a Charis small group. Imagine a funeral in which the mourners tell a young widow that she should start dating soon or join a support group when what she really needs is to have others simply be present to support her as she experiences grief and loss. The purpose of small groups is to provide that supportive presence, enabling each person's words to be heard and held with compassion.

Advice-giving does not require compassion. It moves the conversation from the heart to the head and shifts the focus from the person sharing to the person giving advice. Also, it sets the advice-giver apart as more knowledgeable than the one who has made himself or herself vulnerable.

Finally, advice-giving is often unhelpful or simply wrong, as only the person living the experience can truly understand it. Advice-giving skips the journey of the passion in order to force a premature resurrection. In a small group, the opportunity to be heard with understanding, compassion, and care is what helps retreatants the most.

The Life Cycle of Small Groups

Small groups within a Charis retreat usually follow a predictable cycle with various levels of depth and intimacy and a different focus for each movement of the retreat. For ease of illustration, the following discussion describes the life of a Charis small group over the course of a weekend, but the same principles hold true for shorter Charis events as well.

Initial Small-Group Sessions

The first small group on Friday night meets for a relatively brief time. Its purpose is to introduce group members to one another, break the ice, and begin to create a safe climate that might give rise to deeper sharing at future meetings.

The group begins with introductions that give members the chance to learn basic information about one another. They then share the fruits of their reflection from the quiet time that preceded group time. The reflection questions based on the first talk asks members to name several significant events that shaped their lives in positive ways. This direction helps retreatants begin to share part of their lives while remaining relatively upbeat. The goal is to begin an authentic conversation without going too deep too soon. To find its rhythm, the small group usually depends heavily on the facilitator in the first couple of sessions. The facilitator sets the ground rules and goes first in sharing, modeling the duration and depth that the rest of the group should aim for.

Midway Through the Retreat

Gradually over the next day, the session times are longer and the questions cover a broader range of experiences. The group takes on a life of its own and usually depends less on the facilitator to initiate the sharing. By Saturday evening, the small groups are usually able to focus on some of the deeper challenges of members' lives: places of hurt within relationships, grief and loss, sinfulness, suffering, and searching. The Saturday-evening small group leads naturally into Saturday night's service of healing and reconciliation, where retreatants can bring their lives into Christ's saving embrace through sacramental reconciliation, healing prayer, quiet contemplation, and the song and prayer of the entire retreat community.

Winding up Small-Group Sessions

The small group on Sunday morning changes focus and begins to prepare retreatants for the journey back into daily life. The discussions center on discerning and following our deepest desires and on putting faith into action in a world that badly needs our embrace. The last small-group meetings offer retreatants an opportunity to name the gifts of the retreat, share spontaneous prayer with one another, and bless one another for the journey outward. The goals of the Sunday-morning groups are to bring the retreat and the small groups to closure, to name with gratitude the gifts experienced over the weekend, and to celebrate together.

Maintaining the Flow

Because the small groups are designed to deepen in trust and openness over the weekend, the ideal group has the same membership throughout the retreat. Therefore, we do not rearrange the small groups for each session, though some retreatants might make the retreat in hopes of meeting new people. We respond to this request by explaining our rationale for keeping groups the same and suggesting alternative ways to meet others, such as moving around at various meals or decorating name tags to invite questions.

Sometimes young adults with busy schedules ask to participate in only part of the retreat and to join in a small group. These requests are weighed carefully in light of competing values. In general, we suggest that a small group not contain more than one part-time retreatant. Furthermore, we allow it only if the person is leaving the retreat early, not if he or she is arriving later in the retreat, after the group has already met and begun to build community and trust.

Problems Within Small Groups

Leading and participating in small groups is rewarding work, but it is work nonetheless. Each person must give attention to deciding what part of his or her story to tell, to sharing the story, and to listening attentively as others do the same. Sometimes the challenge increases when a small group encounters particular difficulties. For example, a group member may consistently ignore time limits, sidetrack the group into irrelevant areas, melt down emotionally, or be noncooperative or antagonistic.

Each problem is unique, so we train leaders on how to handle a wide variety of situations. In general, however, we suggest escalating levels of intervention. The first step might be to reiterate the purpose of the small group and the ground rules for functioning. Another step is to call for a break, enabling the leader to speak privately to the person or persons involved or to obtain assistance or consultation from another team member. Finally, an experienced pastoral minister might be asked to deal with the situation outside the group so that the rest of the participants can stay on track.

Within Charis retreats, we make every effort to maintain a safe and healthy atmosphere, and we try not to push buttons that are likely to cause emotional harm. Sometimes, however, despite these efforts, someone does experience a complete emotional meltdown. In this situation, we would not use escalating levels of intervention. Instead, the group leader should

- call for a break in the group time;

- stay with the person and provide emotional support; and

- help him or her to connect with a trained pastoral minister outside the group setting.

Once the group reconvenes, the other group members should be reassured and encouraged to pray for that person.

The entire team can also be a valuable resource for assisting the small-group process. The team holds responsibility for shepherding the retreat as a whole, so leaders should report regularly on small-group progress at team meetings without violating the confidentiality of the group members, except in the most difficult circumstances. The team might help by adjusting the schedule or content if common themes from small groups warrant it. For example, adjustments can be made for more downtime or quiet time if retreatants express that they feel rushed, or brighter lighting and more upbeat music can be added if the group as a whole seems overburdened. Additionally, if retreatants are in need of special attention or care, it may help to inform other team members. Finally, team members can support one another with care, concern, and the wealth of resources and experiences they bring to the retreat.

Conclusion

On retreatants' evaluations, it is not uncommon to find small groups rated among the most valuable elements of the Charis event. Sometimes groups reconvene for reunions. Sometimes new friendships form. Sometimes group pictures are taken. Because of the potential power of small groups, much attention is devoted to training the team in group-facilitation skills prior to the retreat. We have even offered stand-alone workshops in facilitating small faith-sharing groups for all who might want to lead Charis retreats as well as for those who wish to develop these skills for involvement in parishes, organizations, school, or work. (See the retreat resource books for more on small groups.)

It seems appropriate to conclude this discussion with the story of one Charis small group that demonstrated the power of this weekend community to truly become church for one another. At the conclusion of the retreat, the retreat leader introduced the final-blessing ritual. He invited each small-group leader to lay his or her hands on the head and to pray a blessing over each of the six or so members of his or her small group. After the leaders' blessings, the ritual was to conclude and all the group members were to gather in the dining room for lunch. But the members of one group informed the retreat leader that they wanted each group member to bless the others in his or her own words. In spite of time constraints, the members stood firm and insisted on having it their way. Thus, each member pronounced a blessing over all the other group members. After the ritual ended and the rest of the retreatants were well into lunch, this group finished its total of more than thirty blessings. Then the group was ready to join the rest of the retreatants for lunch, and all rejoiced with them at the strong and steadfast "church" they had become. ⚴

CHAPTER 8

Offering Spiritual Resources

The Jesuit spiritual teacher Anthony de Mello recounted a familiar story of a young spiritual seeker who comes to the master asking to learn to pray. The master takes him down to the river and plunges his head into the water. Thinking that this is some novel reminder of baptism, the seeker willingly participates until the master holds his head under the water longer than he expects. Gasping for breath, the seeker angrily demands from the master an explanation. "When your desire for God is as strong as your desire for breath," explains the master, "then will you learn to pray."

Desire for God is the starting place for finding God. This desire to make contact with the Holy is shrouded in the mystery of how God is uniquely alive in each person's heart. We begin by recognizing that prayer cannot really be taught; we can only explain its outer forms. Our task on retreats is to stoke the flames of desire for God, to encourage young adults that such a relationship with God is very possible. The retreat team brings to the retreat its own active faith that God is alive in the world. The team cannot reveal this mystery, but it can point to it and bear witness to it. We hope that the forms of prayer presented in this chapter will help facilitate a process of effectively revealing our faith to others.

The spiritual resources of Charis retreats include ancient and modern forms of prayer, individual spiritual direction, healing prayer, the sacrament of reconciliation, eucharistic adoration, and eucharistic liturgy.

These forms of prayerful contemplation help retreatants bring their life issues directly to God. They invite God to break through into the life of the retreatant and the retreat community in powerful, palpable ways. Additionally, these spiritual resources enable young adults to learn and apply new ways to pray, new understandings of Christian and Catholic traditions, and a new awareness of God's action in their everyday lives.

Prayer Support

As people of faith, it is always important to remember to ask other Christians to pray for the team and for the retreatants during the retreats. Write to local monasteries, abbeys, oratories, and convents to ask for prayer. Ask for prayer from the parish or Newman Center, or from other members of the young adult ministry. Prayer support makes a difference. We are not concerned only with human dynamics; we are engaged in the process of conversion. As Paul writes in Ephesians 6, there are unseen spiritual forces at work in all our lives. Muster all the prayer power you can for the retreat.

The team meetings scheduled throughout the weekend are great opportunities to make time for prayer. We encourage you to begin or to end each of these meetings with a brief prayer. We also recommend that the team gather before each presenter's talk to pray for that person. Invite the speaker to stand in the center of a team circle. If the team member is comfortable with the gesture, lay hands on him or her and invite two or three members to voice spontaneous prayers for the person. We usually conclude with a single verse of a blessing song.

Entering into Sacred Silence

Whether attending a weekend retreat or a single day of prayer, entering into the sacred silence is vital. Unless the young adults can wade into the sacred waters of silence, they will never be able to dive deeply into the pool of God's grace. There are many factors in our overstimulated society that contradict the idea of embracing quiet time. On Friday night, as people arrive at the retreat, they are reminded to turn off their cell phones and pagers, and laptops. A gentle reminder to limit even the spiritual reading is given, for quiet is not only external, but also internal. Coming into the quiet of the Lord is a disciplined, countercultural choice in today's noisy world.

In short, this is a weekend for listening—listening to the speakers' reflections, listening during small-group sharing, listening in the Scriptures proclaimed throughout the retreat, listening in the mystery of the sacraments celebrated, and listening in the quiet of one's room. Facilitating this listening allows us to better hear what God is saying. Just as a cell phone can find us anywhere in the country and bring us a message, so God's call is coming to all those willing to listen for its distinctive ring. You might use these or similar words to discuss sacred silence with the retreatants:

- While complete silence and listening to the Spirit throughout a week or weekend are the norm for Ignatian retreats, Charis retreats introduce silence to mostly first-time retreatants in small increments. Whether in the period from evening prayer until breakfast or the silent reflection period after talks, retreatants are given opportunities to adjust to the quiet and to begin to benefit from it.

- A person sitting alone doesn't necessarily want someone to come up and start talking to him or her. All should respect others' need for silence and space. Allow other participants to experience silence and solitude without interruption.

- Retreatants have varying needs. Some may want to socialize; others may seek quiet or sleep—even during the day. Individual reflection times are periods of silence. Over meals and after evening prayer, the dining room will be designated as the social area; the chapel and bedroom areas and hallways should be kept quiet at all times.

- Silent-reflection times after the presentations can be used in a variety of ways. Using the reflection questions posed by the speaker, retreatants may write down reflections or pray over their responses to the questions. They may contemplate their responses while walking the grounds, sitting in the chapel, or visiting another space in the retreat house. They may use materials (paints, chalks, crayons, clay, and so on) to represent their responses artistically. They may also spend the time in silent prayer for whatever is in their hearts or share their thoughts with a spiritual director.

Prayer in the Great Outdoors

If the retreat house is blessed to be in a great location surrounded by the beauty of nature, then encourage the retreatants to take advantage of the grounds. A small-group session or morning-prayer service could be held outdoors.

Outdoor prayer poses a number of unique challenges, from bugs to breezes to lumpy ground. The acoustics are not great, and it is often hard to stay focused on an in-depth presentation. Carefully consider all the pitfalls before deciding to hold talks outside. Nevertheless, with a bit of forethought and an adventurous spirit, praying outdoors can be uniquely powerful. Simply walking quietly in nature has been all but lost for many young adults. Taking the time to listen to the songs of birds greeting the morning or watching the subtle colors of an evening sunset can place us in direct contact with our Creator in a way that no book, talk, or conversation can. If the heart of contemplation is to look "long and lovingly at the real,"[1] as Dr. Walter Burghardt, S.J., said, it is crucial to encourage the retreatants to unplug from technology and dial into the magnificence of God's creation.

Praying One-on-One

However powerful a group experience may be, there is no escaping the need for a young adult to be able to enter into a meaningful Spirit-driven conversation with a spiritual mentor. Charis retreats provide this opportunity in two keys ways: spiritual direction and an individual experience of the sacrament of reconciliation.

1. Spiritual Direction

In the course of the retreat, topics may arise that are a bit too intimate to be discussed in a small-group setting. There are also deeply personal issues that a young adult will want to explore in greater depth than a small group allows. For this reason, it is helpful to have on hand throughout the weekend one or two trained spiritual directors with whom the retreatants can meet.

Spiritual direction is a conversation with a trained listener that aims to help a person grow in an affective, conscious, and explicit relationship with God. More simply, it is a conversation about his or her life and how

God fits into it. Spiritual direction is not so much about telling or even teaching a young adult what to do. Instead, the director acts like a midwife in helping to birth the Holy Spirit's action in another's life. St. Ignatius of Loyola, the patron saint of retreats, believed that when someone takes the time to really listen to his or her deepest desires, hopes, dreams, and fears, God will respond by gracing that person with God's own presence. Spiritual direction is about facilitating that listening.

The ideal times for spiritual direction on the Charis weekends are during the times for personal reflection, as well as during the break after lunch. Even twenty-minute sessions, although not very long, can be of enormous help and encouragement to the retreatants. We recommend posting a list so that retreatants can easily sign up for conferences in one or two time periods.

2. Sacrament of Reconciliation

Given today's shortage of priests, it can be difficult to get priests to commit to being available to hear confessions on the retreat. Therefore, we encourage contacting local priests as early as possible to invite their participation by celebrating the Eucharist and hearing confession. (Retired priests or religious-order priests at a local monastery or educational institution often have greater flexibility in their schedules than diocesan clergy have. Often they are happy to help hear confessions if contacted far enough in advance.) Some schedule changes may need to be made to ensure the participation of the priests. Adapt our suggestions to fit the needs and realities of the community.

Saturday Reconciliation Service

In addition to providing the opportunity for individual confession throughout the retreat, we include a ninety-minute reconciliation service in three parts. Most young adults have not experienced the sacrament with any regularity. Some may not have celebrated it since their youth. Before the service, it is helpful to offer a brief explanation of why and how to confess. It is also important to calm fears about being judged and explain some specifics about the rite of confession. Provide a leaflet with the words of the Act of Contrition.

The tone for this celebration should not be overly solemn, nor should it be too casual. It is a celebration of God's grace and mercy. The prayers, readings, music, and attitude of the celebrant should express our confidence in divine mercy. Since St. John's first letter assures us that perfect love casts out all fear (1 John 4:18), the reconciliation service should aim to perfect us in love.

Because the reconciliation service is not a Mass or a prayer form required to be led by clergy, this can be an opportunity for a layperson to preside. Vesting the presider in an alb—the liturgical garment of all the baptized—is a helpful symbol to illustrate the dignity of this celebration and to open up an understanding of the laity's role in leading prayer.

1. The Liturgy of the Word

We use candles to help establish an atmosphere of quiet reflection throughout the service. Tea lights are inexpensive and can be used to dramatically alter the mood. The prayer begins with a procession and an opening song. This is followed by an opening prayer, a Scripture reading that emphasizes God's mercy, and a brief homily that sets the tone for what is to come.

See the corresponding retreat resource book for an outline and a script for the reconciliation service. (Visit www.CharisRetreats.org to download and customize this script.)

2. Celebration of Reconciliation and Healing Prayer

During the reconciliation service, we often invite the retreatants to participate in healing prayer. This is the opportunity to experience a compassionate form of intercessory prayer. Two or three team members pray briefly for the intentions offered by retreatants. (The retreat resource books include a section on how to train the team members for this kind of prayer.)

Young adults often come to reconciliation services more aware of their wounds and hurts than of their sins or transgressions. We encourage retreatants to take advantage of both reconciliation and healing prayer, but to come first to the prayer form that most draws them in. Are they keenly aware of their sin? Then the sacrament of reconciliation is the place to start. Do they have an acute sense of their own fragility? If so, then healing prayer is where to begin. In short, keep in mind that God's grace comes in different ways. A simple explanation of this dynamic at the beginning of the reconciliation service is usually helpful.

Depending on the number of retreatants and confessors available, it may be necessary to remind retreatants that confession is not the time for an extended counseling session. The retreatants should confess their sins without a lot of explanation or elaboration. Likewise, the counsel and penance given should be brief and to the point.

After confessing and/or participating in healing prayer, retreatants are encouraged to light candles (usually tea lights) and place them on the altar. Giving retreatants the opportunity to light candles during the service is another way that they can actively symbolize their participation.

> As is true of any worship experience, music moves the heart in a way that mere words cannot.

3. Closing Prayer and Sending Forth

As the confessions draw to a close, the presider signals for the opening song to begin, which regathers the assembly. (Sometimes a few confessions may be continuing as the third part begins.) The community recites together a communal prayer of thanksgiving for God's mercy. There is a closing prayer, some brief announcements about the schedule, an invitation to the ice-cream social, and a closing blessing and recessional song.

Celebrating the Eucharist

The Eucharist is the heart of Catholic worship. If celebrated well, the Eucharist will have a powerful impact on the dynamics of the retreat. Usually, there are two Masses celebrated on Charis retreats—a low-key Eucharist on Saturday and a fuller celebration to close the retreat on Sunday. There are several key components that you will need to consider in order to enhance the celebration.

1. Presider

It is vital to the success of the retreat that the presider is someone who can relate well with young adults as part of the team. This is crucial. It is ideal to have the presider be present for the entire weekend. If that is not possible, it is acceptable to have his participation just for the reconciliation service and the closing Eucharist.

2. Music

As is true of any worship experience, music moves the heart in a way that mere words cannot. Another important consideration is whether to invite a gifted musician to lead the singing throughout the weekend. (When all else fails, resort to singing along with recorded music. But this should be avoided if possible.) Provide worship aids, song sheets, or songbooks so that the assembly can join in the singing.

3. Role of the Assembly

Catholic worship involves participation. Do not turn it into a spectator sport in which a gifted musician and a dynamic presider dominate as everyone else watches. Make sure the lectors, eucharistic ministers, servers, and gift bearers are chosen well before the celebration. It is not uncommon for people to volunteer for the first time for one of these ministries while on retreat. Give them the training needed to perform their roles well.

4. Teaching

"Presume little, explain lots" is the operating principle of the Young Adult Ministry Office of the Archdiocese of Chicago. This is especially true when it comes to liturgy. Many young adults are clueless when it comes to the meaning behind the symbols of the Mass. They are at a loss to explain the structure of the Mass or the layout of the lectionary.

Therefore, at a retreat liturgy, it is often helpful to build in enough time for the presider to do a teaching Mass, interspersing brief explanations of the meaning of certain parts of the liturgy as they occur. Young adults are often hungry for this kind of knowledge, and they greatly appreciate it. But don't overdo it, a little explanation goes a long way.

5. Scripture and Homily

During the homily, it is usually helpful to recap the major themes of the talks the retreatants heard. Ideally, the presider can make a connection between the readings and the themes of the retreat.

In the second half of the homily, we encourage the small groups to have a short, final sharing session. One way to do this is to have team members who are not involved in the small groups label the chairs in the chapel room ahead of time (Susan's group, Bob's group, and so on). When the group enters the chapel for the Eucharist, they move to these assigned seats. After the homily, the presider invites the groups to form small circles. As they do so, the retreatants are invited to briefly name the grace, or charis, they received over the weekend. When everyone has shared, they open the circle and return to their normal seating.

6. Final Blessings/Sending Forth

The Mass proceeds as usual until the final blessing. At this point, the presider invites the small-group leaders forward. Then he hands them small crosses, pins, or other symbolic reminders of the retreat. These are blessed by the presider and then given individually to the retreatants by their small-group leaders. While doing this, the leader prays a short blessing prayer for the individual. Ideally, the prayer is individually tailored, responding in some way to the grace that the retreatant named.

 See the retreat resource books for additional information on the Mass and final blessing.

Prayer Service and Methods

The following prayer methods have been especially useful in helping retreatants enter into the sacred nature of Charis retreats. Additional resources on these prayer methods are found in the retreat resource books.

1. The Examen

St. Ignatius Loyola believed that one of the most important prayers a religious seeker could pray is the daily *examen*, an examination of conscience or consciousness. This prayer involves taking a few minutes once a day to review the thoughts, feelings, and actions that surfaced in the course of the day. The basic questions to ask are "Which of these experiences led me toward God?" and "Which of these led me away from God?" (The retreat resource books contain a method for presenting a guided group form of this prayer. The resource books also include an article on an approach to the *examen* that we have found helpful.)

2. Guided Imagery Prayer

St. Ignatius also taught us about the power of using our imagination in prayer. For example, read the Scripture story from Luke 19:1–10, imagining yourself as Zacchaeus. Experience the sights, sounds, smells, questions, and feelings that Zacchaeus might have experienced. Most young adults have never experienced this kind of prayer, and it is usually met with great enthusiasm. (See the retreat resource books for scripts for this style of meditation.)

3. Lectio Divina, or a Prayerful Reading of the Scriptures

Many young Catholics still have little or no appreciation for the power of God's word. Still others who have studied the word in Scripture courses or in Bible studies have an academic understanding but no idea how to actually pray with the Bible. As an optional prayer experience on some of the Charis retreats, we offer a simple *lectio divina*, a Latin term that means "divine reading." Following is a brief explanation of this method. (See the retreat resource books for a script.)

> St. Ignatius was a great experimenter when it came to prayer.

The young adults are divided into groups of three or four. A leader slowly and prayerfully reads aloud a short passage of Scripture four times. After the first reading, the leader pauses and asks the group to name a word or phrase that struck them. After the second reading, they are asked to name an emotion they felt after hearing the text. Following the third reading, they voice how the passage challenges them in their lives today. During the fourth reading, they are invited to enter into the passage imaginatively, playing the role of a character in the story. When the reading has finished, members of each group may choose to share some part of their prayer experience. Each group concludes with a short, spontaneous prayer offered by group members who feel moved to pray aloud.

This highly structured prayer experience helps the young adults begin to appreciate the power of praying with God's word. It teaches a simple technique that can be applied to their own individual prayer times. Finally, it helps the young adults articulate a connection between the Bible and their own life experiences.

4. Taizé Prayer

Friday night, Saturday morning, and Sunday morning provide opportunities for brief prayer services to close the evening or begin the day. The retreat resource books provide possible scripts for these prayer services. We recommend that at least one of these prayer services use a significant amount of Taizé music. This style of music is easily sung and often helps stir the emotions and soften the heart. We also recommend a generous use of candles to set the mood.

5. Movement Prayer

Many young adults do not understand the importance of gesture, posture, and breath in their prayer. Doing some simple movements, led by a person familiar with movement meditation, can be very helpful. Believers from Eastern religious traditions are accomplished at incorporating movement into their prayer, as with tai chi or walking meditations. These spiritual practices offer a model for Catholic Christians who desire to offer prayer and praise by making full use of the bodies God has "so wonderfully" made. (Psalm 139:14) Gesturing or dancing to religious music can also be quite powerful. Young adults are often open to this style of prayer if it is not too complicated and is well explained.

A Fresh Experience of Traditional Devotions

Young adults today often have little experience with the rich devotional life of the Church. Using a meditation on the sign of the cross or praying the rosary or the chaplet of divine mercy can be powerful. The key to increasing receptivity for today's young adults is to explain and present these prayers properly. Anything that smacks of rote, mindless ritual is deadly! See the retreat resource books for more on these prayers.

We often incorporate eucharistic adoration into some retreats and occasionally have included an all-night vigil, inviting the young adults to sign up to pray before the Blessed Sacrament in half-hour increments. Many young adults who have never previously prayed this way have reported sensing a spiritual presence and a deep calm during these prayers.

Conclusion

St. Ignatius was a great experimenter when it came to prayer. He kept copious notes on what he found to be helpful for himself and for others. He had all kinds of suggestions and a fairly well-defined structure for his school of meditation. For St. Ignatius, the bottom line was always about stopping and praying where the grace was found. Plan what to pray about, but in a given moment, always adapt to the graces being given.

Charis retreats are about going into the storehouse of our tradition, like the wise master of the household who brings forth from his treasury both the old and new. (Matthew 13:52) Some traditional Catholic practices can be brought forward to today's young adults with much spiritual profit. We also encourage you to continue to experiment with new ways of praying with retreatants. ⚭

CHAPTER 9

After the Retreat: Journeys Ended, Journeys Begun

For Christians, the power of the Gospel does not end with the resurrection and ascension of Jesus. Rather, the sacred story lives on in those who receive the gifts of God's spirit and who follow Christ's great commission to "Go . . . and make disciples of all nations . . . And . . . I am with you always, until the end of the age." (Matthew 28:19–20)

Similarly, the power of encountering God's spirit on a Charis retreat does not end when young adults receive the final blessing at Mass, finish lunch, and drive out the driveway. Rather, as the weekend winds down and in the days and weeks afterward, the gifts of the retreat can continue into each young adult's everyday life. Ideally, the experience of Charis ripples outward, with each retreatant and team member living out the graces of the weekend, touching other lives, and perhaps even inviting others to be part of a Charis retreat. In that way, Charis participants take an active role in living out the great commission, with Christ present every step of their way.

This chapter will focus on three aspects of building the bridge outward from the Charis retreat weekend. First, we'll consider how the retreat itself is brought to closure. Second, we'll address reasons and methods for evaluating the retreat. Finally, we'll look at ways of continuing the spirit of a Charis retreat in the weeks and months that follow.

Winding Up the Retreat

At the risk of sounding like a Caribbean cruise commercial, a weekend retreat can be an idyllic experience, a vacation for one's spirit. Retreatants' needs are met from the moment they arrive. While they attend to other activities, their meals are prepared and served, and someone else cleans up. They settle into private rooms where their beds are made up with fresh linens. A fire burns in the fireplace, and soft music plays. For nearly forty-plus hours, retreatants have the chance to rest, recreate, and explore deep places. A caring community engulfs them, and the friendships formed here may last. Life doesn't get much better than this.

Some would consider the transition out of such a weekend almost as jarring as ejection from the womb. Many young adults are returning to homes they occupy alone, some are returning to a less-than-fulfilling work life, and all are going back to the struggles and blessings of the everyday. In light of this, the team has an ethical responsibility to help people weather the transition out of the retreat and to bring the gathered community to gentle closure.

The outward focus of Sunday morning sets the stage for winding down the weekend. The talk, reflection questions, and small-group sessions all begin to prepare retreatants to return to daily life. The topics lead young adults to consider their mission to the world beyond themselves and beyond the safe container of the retreat, as well as to name and share the gifts the weekend has given them.

Retreat is a time that can bring about conversion, a change of heart. Therefore, it is important to invite young adults in the final hours to consider things within the world and within themselves that they may feel called to try to change. The final talk and reflection questions focus on mission and putting one's faith into action in the wider world and in daily life. This is an ideal time for retreatants to set their intentions toward some concrete action to continue the experience: perhaps to pray more frequently, get involved in young adult ministry, volunteer with those who are homeless, work harder on a relationship, or explore a different career path. Much of the conversation, prayer, and blessing of the final hours are geared toward articulating the new path ahead and supporting young adults as they step into it.

During the final small-group sessions, retreatants are invited to name the gifts of the retreat for themselves and for one another. Maybe a gift was newfound courage to take on a particular challenge. Maybe it was healing, inner peace, or movement out of isolation. Perhaps the gift was a new friendship formed, a deer spotted in the trees, or awareness of being held and loved by God. In small groups and at the closing Mass, retreatants are also invited to pray together—thanking God for these gifts, anticipating and asking for what they will need as they depart, and blessing one another for the road ahead. In this way, retreatants conclude the weekend deliberately and with celebration. Hugs, tears, laughter, and group snapshots often punctuate the concluding moments.

Evaluating the Experience

Evaluation is another important way for retreatants and team members alike to name the gifts of the weekend and to incorporate them into lessons for life and ministry. Although work and school experiences cause some to dread or dismiss evaluations as superfluous, their significance as a tool for reflection, learning, and shaping the Charis program cannot be overstated.

1. Retreatant Evaluations

Evaluation forms should be brief, asking a few questions to gather specific input about the retreat. An evaluation form is included in the retreat resource books.

> Visit **www.CharisRetreats.org** to download and customize the evaluation form.

The form should take no more than five or ten minutes to complete. The most candid evaluations provide for anonymity; therefore, a form seeking to gauge someone's interest in serving on the team or being on a contact list should be separate from the evaluation itself or be part of a tear-off section.

> **This type of question plants the seed for retreatants to begin to consider other Charis involvement beyond the weekend.**

Evaluations get the fullest responses when they are completed after most retreat activities have concluded but before people are going out the door. One good time is after Sunday liturgy but before lunch.

A well-placed introduction and statement of rationale can increase the quantity and quality of forms received. The leader might mention that the evaluation fulfills the spiritual value of looking deeply at the retreat experience and naming the gifts and challenges. The leader can also request young adults' help in creating future Charis programs by providing honest feedback about what worked well for them, what needed improvement, and what other areas Charis might develop. A marked box or basket for completed evaluations should be prominently placed where people are exiting the room for lunch. Although the end of the retreat is usually a bit rushed, making quality time for evaluations while retreatants are still a captive audience is nonetheless important for each retreatant and for Charis overall.

The specific evaluation form and questions can vary according to the type of Charis program as well as the needs of a particular locale. Generally, we ask retreatants to list three aspects of the retreat that worked well. Similarly, we ask what can be improved. Finally, we direct specific questions to areas we want to know more about. For example, we might ask retreatants to rate the amount of free time they had over the weekend: Too much/too little/about right.

Evaluations also serve as a means of gathering information for Charis leaders about the Catholic young adults who participate. We ask retreatants how they heard about the weekend, which lets us know which marketing approaches work best. We also use the form to test-market interest in other types of Charis programs. This can be done with a question such as "Please check any of the following Charis programs you might be interested in attending," followed by a list that includes retreat follow-up evening, day of reflection, volunteer service day, week-long mission trip, silent directed retreat from one to eight days, weekend or program for couples, week-long pilgrimage, small-group faith sharing, afternoon church tour, and spiritual book club, and so on. This type of question plants the seed for retreatants to begin to consider other Charis involvement beyond the weekend and enables Charis leaders to plan future programs that might be well attended.

Charis leaders should also gather some demographic data about retreatants, such as age, marital status, gender, ethnicity, and home parish if any. Because race and ethnicity questions can be offensive to some, this data can be gathered by interacting with the attendees instead of through a form question. Charis leaders can use demographic data to learn better who is being served and what needs remain unmet. Additionally, parish information can indicate which are the most young adult-friendly parishes in a city or region so that Charis can hold or promote programs there or can refer young adults seeking a parish home. (On several Seekers' Retreats, half the young adult attendees listed no home parish affiliation.)

2. Team Evaluations

An evaluation of a retreat weekend by the team members is every bit as important as the one by the retreatants. Because the team members possess intimate knowledge of how the retreat unfolded, both in its public face and behind the scenes, they are in a position to offer valuable commentary and suggestions. Furthermore, the team evaluation helps team members debrief after what is often an intense experience for them. Discussion can surface and solidify what they have learned about how to do effective ministry. They can also reflect on themselves as ministers and church leaders—the gifts they bring, areas they need to develop, and ways they have grown and changed.

We recommend that the team evaluation take place in two parts. The first would occur on-site immediately after the retreat ends, while the experience is still fresh but before distance has permitted deeper reflection. Team members read the evaluations together, and then they discuss three questions:

1. What did you see as the gifts of this retreat? What worked well?

2. What could have been better—areas for improvement?

3. Among the retreatants, especially those in your small groups, whom would you recommend to lead a future Charis weekend?

The final team meeting also serves as a chance to tie up any loose ends that may linger from the dynamics of the weekend. This meeting has been a place to resolve conflict among team members, to discern a need to follow up with a particular retreatant, and to discuss issues that have arisen out of, for example, race or gender differences. At last, the final team meeting is a chance to pray together and to celebrate hard work and a job well done. This meeting may even lead to an optional meeting-after-the-meeting at someone's house for food and continuing conversation.

The second part of the team evaluation takes place at least a couple weeks after the retreat, when the experience has had a chance to sink in and take root. Team members often gel into a community in the course of planning and giving the retreat, so they welcome the chance to reunite later. Typically, the gathering includes a potluck or other dinner at someone's house. The evening can include shared prayer, as well as conversation about what memories of the retreat are especially striking now. In this meeting, we again ask team members to share anything they may have learned about ministry or themselves as ministers. Small gifts such as neck crosses, books, or icons are presented as mementos. These kinds of keepsakes are available from Catholic bookstores or online.

Helping People Make Connections After the Retreat

Charis weekend retreats, wonderful though they are, should not exist in isolation. They are not intended to serve as a one-stop oasis in the desert, feeding Catholic young adults briefly in an environment where nothing else is available for them. Anyone who sets out to offer one Charis weekend without any follow-up or effort to connect with the broader church should be strongly discouraged. A Charis weekend without follow-up or some sort of continuity risks doing more harm than good by falsely raising young adults' hopes that the local church is interested in ministering with and incorporating them.

Therefore, the importance of helping those who attend Charis weekends to make continuing ministry connections cannot be emphasized enough. Leaders have a responsibility to enable Charis participants to connect with one another after the retreat and also to connect with the larger church and civic community. The U.S. bishops articulated this philosophy in their 1997 pastoral letter *Sons and Daughters of the Light*.[1] They stated the following goals for Catholic young adult ministry:

- Connect young adults with Jesus Christ.

- Connect young adults with the Catholic Church.

- Connect young adults with the mission of the church in the world.

- Connect young adults with one another.

The first way to maintain connections and continuity is to gather and save information from those who attend a Charis weekend. This includes contact information such as name, address, phone, and e-mail. Contact information is important so that Charis can let attendees know about future programs and opportunities. This information is also valuable to provide to the retreatants so that they can contact one another and have small-group reunions. At the same time, to safeguard privacy, no contact information about any retreatant should be given to another without that retreatant's permission. Also, all who receive contact information should be advised of the importance of protecting retreatants' privacy. For example, retreatants and team members should not give out others' e-mail addresses without permission.

In addition to gathering and disseminating retreatant contact information, Charis leaders can also help keep the retreat experience alive by offering follow-up programs. Ideally, a follow-up takes place a few weeks after the retreat weekend, when the experience is still fresh. Retreatants are invited to bring friends, whether or not the friends have made a Charis retreat. The experience is a great way to reunite retreatants and to expose newcomers to a small taste of Charis.

A follow-up can be like a mini-Charis evening that includes some of the elements of the retreat, such as a talk or panel presentation, small-group conversation, and group prayer. Conversation starters can include "What strikes you most about your retreat experience?" or "What effect did the retreat have on you, both on the weekend and in the days and weeks since then?"

In Cincinnati, we have held follow-ups on Friday evenings after work, ordering in pizza and soft drinks for supper. The time offers a substantive alternative to happy hour in a bar and also enables attendees to head out later together if they wish. A downtown parish anxious to draw young adults willingly provided its facilities for the follow-ups; it even provided its keyboardist to lead the group in song. Recent retreatants were tapped to help plan and present the evening.

● ● ● ● ● ● ● ● ● ● ● ● ● ● ● ● ● ●

Make information about other ministry and service opportunities available to retreatants.

● ●

Charis follow-ups can also occur at times of special need. One such evening took place in the immediate aftermath of September 11. Retreatants welcomed the opportunity to tap into a supportive community, to share and pray together in a difficult moment. A follow-up also occurred as the whole diocese was preparing to celebrate the feast of Our Lady of Guadalupe with the Hispanic community. The follow-up evening enabled young adults to learn about the feast and what it might mean in their own lives, preparing them for meaningful participation in the larger event.

A final way to maintain the bridge between a Charis weekend and the larger faith community is to make information about other ministry and service opportunities available to retreatants. On weekend retreats, we have a literature table displaying material such as the *Response* directory of volunteer opportunities from the Catholic Network of Volunteer Service, material about religious and lay ministry vocations, and ministry-training programs in the area. In each retreatant's folder, we also provide the following:

- A list of young adult ministries. These include Charis programs, diocesan young adult ministry, young adult-friendly parishes and groups. Information also includes upcoming programs, meeting times and dates, locations, Web sites, and contact information.

- Links to national Web sites such as www.CharisMinistries.org and www.CharisPartners.org. The Charis Partner site provides links to the sites of www.BustedHalo.com—the Paulist Fathers' young adult ministry—and the National Catholic Young Adult Ministry Association at www.ncyama.org.

- Information about local volunteer services, such as tutoring and soup kitchens. These enable retreatants to offer their gifts to the larger community, sometimes while connecting with faith-based organizations.

- Spiritual direction and counseling resources. These give retreatants the opportunity to continue and perhaps intensify the interior work began on the retreat.

All this information, however, is not simply tucked away in a folder or set on a table. Instead, the retreat team calls attention to it both in the introductory session as well as at the final lunch before departure.

The final lunch also allows team members and retreatants to make announcements to the whole group about young adult ministries they are involved with, upcoming events, and so on. The retreat folders and lunchtime announcements should invite retreatants to the next Charis follow-up and provide the date, time, and location. A later group e-mail can reiterate the follow-up invitation.

Conclusion

In sum, the Charis retreat experience should be a living one that does not end when the weekend concludes. The team should take care to help retreatants name the gifts of the retreat so that these gifts take root. Additionally, the team should work to bring the retreat to a healthy close while preparing retreatants to go and live the mission of Christ and the graces of the retreat in daily life.

The evaluation process is one way to help the retreat live and grow. Retreatants and team members alike are invited to share their experiences of what went well on the weekend, what should be changed, and what other programs they would like to see Charis offer. Team evaluations enable team members to articulate what they have learned about ministry and about themselves as ministers and leaders.

Another way to keep the spirit of a Charis weekend alive is to help people make connections after the retreat. Dissemination of team and retreatant contact information enables people to stay in touch and get together later. (It is important, however, to build in procedures that honor and safeguard retreatants' privacy.) Team members and retreatants can also plan follow-up programs that serve as retreat reunions. Finally, retreatant folders, a literature table, and Sunday lunchtime announcements can invite retreatants to try out other regional young adult ministries, other Charis programs, volunteer service, religious and lay ministry vocations, and spiritual direction or counseling. In all these ways, the Spirit continues to lead, and the graces of the retreat live on and multiply. ⚁

Adaptations of Charis Programs

The needs and availability of young adults can vary greatly. For these reasons, Charis has developed several adaptations to its programs as well as opportunities for extended silent, individually directed retreats. These include day-long activities, single overnight retreats, and different weekend retreat models. In this chapter and in the companion chapters in the retreat resource books, we will outline some of the Charis models and provide materials that enable readers to adapt Charis programs to their settings.

The Seekers' Retreat

Dynamics and Theme

Building on the "seek and you will find; knock and the door will be opened to you" passage from Matthew 7:7, the theme of the Seekers' Retreat is one of welcoming the person who is looking for more—more understanding, more connection with one's values, more faith, more of a relationship with God or the Catholic community, or perhaps more quiet from a noisy, overcommitted young adult life.

The Charis Seekers' Retreat is generally considered the first in our series, but it is not necessary for participants to begin with this retreat before participating in the others. Young adults are at varying points in their spiritual journeys; you may find that a community is less interested in the Seekers' Retreat and more drawn to another model. In this case, you are certainly not bound to begin with the Seekers' Retreat.

The length of the retreat is another variable open to your discretion. While we designed the Seekers' model for a weekend retreat, we recognize that financial or pastoral considerations may lead retreat ministers to abbreviate the program to a single day.

The retreat dynamic for this retreat, as outlined in Chapter 3, begins with hospitality and welcome to a retreatant whom we assume is a newcomer to faith and perhaps nervous about attending a weekend-long religious program. Keeping that spirit of hospitality and welcome throughout, the retreatant is led by reassuring team and pastoral staff members into an exploration of experience, tradition, and encounters with the Holy. Through presentations and small-group sharing, peer team members offer increasingly deep reflections. They invite the retreatants to move into the places in their hearts where they have experienced God leading, loving, and healing them. The end goal is for retreatants to understand how

Sample Charis Seekers' Retreat Schedule

The Search for Faith
Friday, May 14–Sunday, May 16

Friday *My past: Where have I come from? Where have I found God in my life?*

3:00–6:55	Registration
7:00	Table blessing, dinner, introductions, welcome
8:00	Prologue: Why Are You Here?
	Presentation: Knowing Ourselves—Our Faith Stories
	Personal activity (silence)
	Small-group sharing
	Short break
10:15	Meditation
	Retire

Saturday *My present: Where am I now? Where do I find God in my life?*

7:00	Wake-up bell
7:30–8:30	Breakfast
8:30	Prayer
	Announcements
	Presentation: Naming What's Important
	Personal activity (silence)
	Small-group sharing
11:30	Lunch, free time, individual conferences (optional)
2:30	Presentation: *Examen, Discernment, and Prayer in Everyday life*
	Personal activity (silence)
	Small-group sharing
	Short break

5:00	Liturgy
6:00	Dinner
7:00	Presentation: Suffering, Healing, and Hope
	Personal activity (silence)
	Small-group sharing
	Short break
9:00	Celebration of the sacrament of reconciliation
10:30	Retire or ice-cream social (optional) or individual conferences (optional)

Sunday *My future: What is my deepest desire? What is God's invitation to me?*

7:00	Wake-up bell
7:30–8:25	Breakfast
8:30	Presentation: Our Deepest Desires
	Personal activity (silence)
	Small-group sharing
	Short break
10:30	Liturgy, faith, and community; faith and action; missioning
12:00	Sharing and lunch
1:00	Departure

close God has been, is, and will be throughout their lives.

Peers offer presentations beginning with "Knowing Ourselves" on Friday night, where retreatants look to the events and people who have shaped their lives to this point. "Naming What's Important" is the second presentation. This is a reflection upon values, relationships, and priorities, including the relationships with God and with a faith community. A presentation on prayer follows, moving retreatants from talking about God to talking with God and naming a unique relationship with God. The fourth presentation, held on Saturday evening on the weekend retreat, invites the retreat community to look at areas of suffering they have experienced and where God has been present as healer and hope. Finally, the last (usually Sunday morning) presentation and following liturgy lead retreatants to recognize God as their ultimate and deepest desire. A sample schedule for the Seekers' Retreat is shown here. See *The Seekers' Retreat Resource Book* for a complete team schedule, one-day and single overnight adaptations of the retreat schedule, preparation materials, and sample scripts.

Throughout the retreat, the pastoral team uses the presentations, prayer services, spiritual-direction time, optional sessions, and informal conversations to offer catechesis and formation in regard to Scripture, prayer, and the Catholic tradition. Formal catechesis is not a part of the small-group sharing session. (See Chapter 7 for guidelines for small groups.)

Who Attends?

Very often, those who attend Seekers' Retreats have never been on a religious retreat, or it is their first retreat as an adult. They often feel on the margins of the Catholic community and may not be regular attendees at Mass. Many have noted that they were brought up Catholic but may not consider themselves practicing Catholics. Yet they are looking for a connection to God (and perhaps to the Church).

Retreatants have learned about retreats from

- young adult friendly parishes or priests;

- Catholic school (high school or college) alumni clubs;

- parents or other guiding figures, including vocation directors of religious communities; and

- peers attending young adult programs (religious, community, or service programs).

Team and Preparation

The team for the Seekers' Retreat consists of one or two pastoral staff members, ideally a collaborative team of priest and laity. These pastoral staff members guide the young adult members, lead prayer and formation/catechesis, and provide spiritual direction and pastoral wisdom to retreatants. At least five prepared-peer team members give talks, facilitate small groups, and lead prayer. (See Chapter 4 for thorough discussions of selecting and preparing team members.)

The Jesus Retreat or "Who Do You Say I Am?" Retreat

The Jesus Retreat is a peer- and pastoral-minister-led weekend retreat with a basic format similar to the Seekers' Retreat. Developed in several stages between 2000 and 2002 by Jesuits, Charis staff, and key young adult volunteers and pastoral ministers in Chicago and Cincinnati, the first model was suggested in an academic paper by Jesuit scholastic Peter Nguyen. He based the model on the weeks of the Spiritual Exercises of St. Ignatius of Loyola. From Nguyen's paper and from the experience and feedback gained from conducting multiple Seekers' Retreats, an initial model was developed for use for April 2002.

Dynamics and Theme

For the Jesus Retreat as first used, the dynamic and talks of the weekend revolve loosely around the weeks of the Exercises and on the text in the Gospel according to Matthew: "But who do you say that I am?" (Matthew 16:15) Retreatants are invited to explore their unique relationship to Jesus. They explore questions such as

- Who was he?
- Who is he for us?
- Where has he been with us on our journey?
- How can we follow him more closely?

Through a series of talks by young adults, reflection periods, small-group sessions, communal and individual prayer, and several other optional activities, retreatants spend the weekend dedicated to answering the question posed to Jesus' disciples, and in the meantime, find themselves enriching their relationship with the Person of Jesus.

The retreat model has been modified in Chicago and Cincinnati to better accommodate perceived pastoral need and young adult passions. For example, while Chicago retreats have maintained a five-talk schedule that initially followed the weeks of the Exercises quite closely, in Cincinnati, the talks' themes have been reworked with input from team members to focus more on how Jesus lives and moves in a particular team member's life. Both cities' pastoral staff take more time with young adult team members to develop their talks and to incorporate both personal experience and the teachings of the church.

See *The Jesus Retreat Resource Book* for preparation materials used by Chicago and by Cincinnati team members as well as for a complete script of the Jesus Retreat.

Who Attends?

We have found that this topic/theme appeals primarily to those who are ready to commit their time and their energy to delving into a living relationship with Jesus. We have found that retreatants often include the following:

- those who came previously to a Seekers' Retreat

- those who may be more attentive in their religious practice (by being regular Mass-goers or members of a parish or faith group)

- those who are looking to get to the root of the Christian message in their own lives

Team Preparation

Finally, due to the deeper theological questions and faith experiences presented by team members, we have found that it pays to give the team longer to prepare for the retreat. The team meetings may follow a schedule similar to that of a Seekers' Retreat, but should be begun earlier in order to allow for more questions and individual consultation with talk mentors. Because this retreat has a catechetical element to it (What does the Church teach about Jesus?), there is more interaction between the young adult team members and a member of the pastoral staff. Before the retreat, this allows for team catechesis and theological integration of the talks. On the retreat itself, each talk is introduced by one of the pastoral ministers, a talk mentor, or another theologically educated person in order to clearly and concisely connect the presenter's experience- and Scripture-based talk with the larger Catholic tradition and theology.

Again, while the retreat was designed to be held over a weekend, the Jesus Retreat has been conducted as a one-day program. On the following page is a sample one-day schedule.

Other Charis Retreat Models

In contrast to the many retreats that are seen as a one-time experience of initiation, Charis retreats are meant to help young adults grow in a variety of topics related to faith and life development. Consequently, we have developed a healthy range of retreat models. This list continues to grow.

As with all Charis interactive retreats, these models highlight personal faith reflections by young adults who are speaking to their peers on topics related to the retreat theme. In addition, a brief teaching point relates the theme to the church's tradition. This is either woven into the talk itself or presented by someone trained in theology and given as a prelude to the talk. Structured periods of silent reflection and small-group sharing are also included.

Besides the Seekers' Retreat and the Jesus Retreat, following are some other Charis retreat models. We hope to make retreat resource books available for these retreats as well.

Called and Chosen: Renewing Our Catholic Commitment

This retreat explores the distinctive elements of the Roman Catholic faith and challenges young adults to seek deep roots within this faith tradition.

The Spirit at Work Within: Discerning Our Gifts

The gifts and charisms given by the Holy Spirit help us find our own unique role within the Body of Christ. Young adults reflect on their own gifts and how these can be used for the benefit of others.

Peace and Justice: Catholic Social Teaching

One of the best-kept secrets of the Catholic Church is the challenge our faith gives us to live the Gospel in service to the poor and to work for a faith that seeks justice. This retreat examines ways to live out our call to work for peace and justice for all God's children.

Sample Charis Jesus Retreat Schedule—One-Day Program

Who Do You Say I Am?
Exploring our Relationship with Jesus
Saturday, November 5

9:00	Arrival and Check-in
9:30	Welcome, Introductions, & Opening Prayer
	Presentation 1: Who do you say I am? Why does it matter?
	Individual Reflection & Quiet Break
	Small-Group Sharing
11:45	Lunch
12:30	Re-Gathering: The People Who Met Jesus
	Presentation 2: Deepening My Friendship with Jesus
	Individual Reflection & Quiet Break
	Small-Group Sharing
2:10	Re-Gathering: Bartimaeus
	Presentation 3: Jesus' Greatest Gift
	Individual Reflection & Quiet Break
	Small-Group Sharing
3:45	Liturgy of the Eucharist
5:00	Evaluation, Acknowledgements, and Departure

Sex in the City of God: Faith, Intimacy, and Relationships

Through Scripture, Church teaching, and the lived experience of young adults, this retreat explores the gift, challenge, and responsibility of human sexuality and the place of conscience in moral decision making.

Decisions! Decisions! and Transitions That Follow

Young adult life is especially filled with significant life decisions that have an impact for years to come. This retreat offers useful tools for exploring the spirituality and psychology of what can often be a stormy journey.

Charis Seasonal and Topical Days of Reflection

Another effective way to reach young adults is through a seasonal or topical day of reflection. These half- or full-day programs can be an effective way to introduce the Charis program to a group or diocese of young adults, since they do not require a full weekend commitment, cost less for planners and participants, and can be an empowering experience for first-time volunteers. Like the weekend retreats, the day-long format consists of presentations, time for individual reflection, small-group sharing, and communal prayer. A day of reflection differs in the following ways.

Length

Day-long Charis days of reflection are generally limited to a 10 A.M. to 4 P.M. time frame. This allows adequate preparation and set-up time for team members in the morning, while allowing young adult participants to sleep in or run errands before the program begins. It also allows for evening activities for all. Many times we have heard of people meeting on the day of prayer and then heading out for social activities together after the program's close. The relatively short day also allows for parents of small children to attend while a spouse or sitter cares for the children.

Team

The main difference in this format is that the team is usually composed of one or two main presenters who are professional speakers or pastoral ministers. Think of speakers who can effectively engage young adults and help them prepare for a Christmas or an Easter event.

If the budget allows for bringing in outside talent, this can be a helpful way to jump-start a program. Speakers, musicians, actors, and other performing artists have proven very effective in helping young adults engage head and heart in pondering questions of faith.

The team also includes a young adult coordinator (either the associate director or an experienced volunteer) as well as young adult volunteers who act as registrants, setup crew, hospitality ministers, small-group facilitators, music ministers, and assistants to the presenters. All but the facilitators and musicians can be trained the morning of the program. This leads to a much lighter time commitment for all while having as few as five and as many as twenty-five volunteers on board for the day and as recruiters prior to the event. Depending on how well established young adult ministry or Charis programs are in the area, even smaller teams for smaller programs can be effective.

Both professional and volunteer team members should commit well in advance of the program—up to a year for the professionals and up to three months for the volunteers.

Facility

Because the program does not require overnight lodging, and only one meal plus snacks (which could be brought by volunteers) is needed, a broad range of facilities will work. Including a reconciliation service or Mass at the end of the day, as is often the case, requires a space that could serve as a chapel. Knowing well in advance what the program will include—such as music, dance, podium, space for movement, worship space, rooms for small groups—allows the coordinator to contract the most suitable facility. We have found success with churches that have multiple break-out rooms (the chapel serving as the main presentation space) and with retreat centers with single-day availability. (The closer the facility is to the concentration of young adults in the area, the greater the attendance.)

> Young adult life is filled with significant decisions that have an impact for years to come.

Logistics

While the program is shorter, the amount of logistics involved in a day of reflection is still substantial. It takes time to identify and secure a team, space, and materials. There is still the investment of time needed for invitations, registration, and pre-program hospitality. Pastoral ministers will need adequate preparation time, and musicians will need to rehearse. Several hours of training for small-group facilitators (if this is their first time in the role) will be required. The setup and teardown can take as much as an hour on either end of the program.

Careful coordination with the facilities' management is required to ensure a seamless program, the comfort of all retreatants, and good relationships for future day-long or weekend programming. It is key for the program's coordinator to keep in close contact with all team members in the weeks prior to the event to make sure they feel prepared, to keep them enthusiastic, and to help them recruit others for participation in the day's program. Above is a sample schedule for a day of reflection. ⚭

Sample Charis Advent Day of Reflection

9:30	Registration: Coffee and donuts
10:00	Opening prayer and Presentation 1
11:00	Private reflection
11:15	Break
11:30	Small-group sharing
12:15	Lunch
1:15	Presentation 2
2:00	Private reflection
2:15	Small-group sharing
2:45	Break
3:00	Reconciliation service (with Liturgy of the Word)
3:30	Confession (with optional healing prayer)
4:15	Closing prayer, wrap up, final announcements, evaluations, and end of the day
4:45	Departure

Conclusion

The word *retreat* in a spiritual context suggests taking time to step back and assess where one is going in life. There is great value in this pursuit. But St. Ignatius of Loyola preferred the term *spiritual exercise* because it suggests building strength for a mission.

Charis weekends and days of prayer are both retreats and spiritual exercises. They are time set apart, sacred time given to our search for the Holy in the midst of an often frenetic pace of life. But they are more.

Matthew's Gospel concludes with the great commission of Jesus sending his disciples to the furthest ends of the earth to proclaim his Good News. Being Catholic and Christian is ultimately about becoming the work of Christ, of renewing the words of Jesus in every generation through the strength of our witness. It is our firm hope and deep prayer that the Charis program will, in fact, be a source of grace and renewal of faith for many young adults across the country. Will you help us in this mission?

Fr. John Cusick, the longtime director of Young Adult Ministry for the Archdiocese of Chicago and a mentor for many of us young adult ministers around the country, has suggested that young adult ministry is like "a floating craps game." By that he means that the locus of this ministry is always shifting. What worked ten years ago isn't necessarily working today. And what works in one part of the country isn't necessarily going to work in another place. The game is the same. The rules and location keep shifting.

In that context, we invite your help and offer ours. Our Web site, www.CharisRetreats.org, will give you more details on becoming part of the Charis Retreat support network, which shares best practices, enables you to learn about alternative models and sample talks, offers suggestions for songs to introduce talks, and provides a wealth of other resources. Tell us and others who choose to become part of the support network what works for your young adults, what adaptations are successful, and what innovations you've made. We're in this work together.

Charis retreats and Days of Prayer may not be the ideal way to begin a young adult ministry in your area. Theology-on-Tap programs, Bible studies, book clubs, evenings of prayer, and special mid-week young adult liturgies are all proven ways of building initial interest. If this is the case, once the group has begun to gel, there will be a desire for something more, a yearning for what comes next. It is at this crucial juncture that the Charis retreat program kicks in.

However, we have also found that sometimes areas void of significant young adult ministry want to jump-start their programs with a Charis weekend retreat or a Charis-style Day of Prayer. Any way you come to Charis, think of us as a spiritual think tank for programs of renewal for young adults.

Let us know how the retreats and spiritual exercises are working in your area. Together let us carry the light of the Lord's love forward into a world groping in shadows for what only Christ can provide! ⚶

Acknowledgments

This retreat guide bears the names of the three people primarily responsible for compiling it: Fr. J. Michael Sparough, S.J., Diane Michutka Fraser, and Mary Anne Reese. However, this guide represents the inspiration and creativity of so many more people who have been part of Charis Ministries over the past eight years.

Charis would not be in existence were it not for the passion for young adult ministry of Fr. Ed Schmidt, S.J., and Fr. Dick Baumann, S.J.— two Jesuit provincials of the Chicago Province whose vision and generosity enabled this ministry to flourish. Scott Opperman, Margaret Ryan, Fr. Mike Conley, S.J., Mary Mathias, and Mike Brennan were all part of the original design team for the first Charis retreats. Matt Paschke first suggested the name Charis. Many young adult team members helped shape the unique Charis approach to young adult ministry. Some of them will be named in the resource books for particular retreats, and many more of them will remain unnamed but were significant contributors to this process.

Although Charis is now based in Chicago, our earlier retreats were jointly developed with a team in Cincinnati. Mary Anne Reese and Fr. Tim Hipskind, S.J., first brought Charis Ministries to Cincinnati. Later, Joan Chidester Stoltz joined them in shaping these retreats.

Jenéne Francis, our Managing Director at Charis, made an enormous contribution to the entire Charis *Grace Notes* series. Through helping to secure funding for the project, test-marketing the manuscript, working with our partners around the country, co-writing some chapters of the resource books and analyzing others, her work helped make this book possible.

We wish to acknowledge our deep gratitude to the folks at BustedHalo .com. Charis Ministries held our first retreat around the same time that the Paulist Young Adult Ministry Office launched its Web site. Mike Hayes and Fr. Brett Hoover, C.S.P., first brought Charis east of the Alleghenies. Later, Fr. Dave Dwyer, C.S.P., joined Mike in continuing Charis retreats on the East Coast.

Lauren Berke, Fr. Michael's assistant, helped duplicate manuscripts, correct copy, and assist with many details. Mary Healy, our amazing Charis volunteer, did the initial sorting for the series manuscripts, helping us organize random stacks of retreat notes and synchronize information stored on different computers with a variety of file names. Carrie Gallagher, Chris Penna, Annie Devine, and Lauren Gaffey at the Charis office all helped move the project to completion.

We are blessed to have these manuals published by Loyola Press. Fr. George Lane, S.J., Terry Locke, and Matthew Diener believed in the value of this project from the start. Their suggestions over the last four years ensured that these books came to light. Our editor, Aaron George, is the very model of a modern, skilled editor. Not content to simply review the manuscript, Aaron, himself a young adult, participated in several Charis events and even joined the team for a recent retreat. He managed to find the right combination of carrot and stick to keep us motivated and on schedule. Aaron was ably assisted by Maggie Hong and Jason Zech from the Loyola Press staff. We also thank copyeditors Beth Renaldi and Diane Gonciarz for their keen attention to detail.

Finally, we want to thank the more than one thousand young adult men and women who have been part of Charis Ministries these past eight years. Their vulnerability in sharing their life stories and their willingness to continue seeking God's grace has brought this ministry to life.

Fr. J. Michael Sparough, S.J.
Diane Michutka Fraser
Mary Anne Reese

Endnotes

Chapter 1

1. U.S. Catholic Bishops. *Sons and Daughters of the Light: A Pastoral Plan for Ministry with Young Adults.* Washington, D.C.: United States Conference of Catholic Bishops, Inc., 1996.

2. Barna, George. *Baby Busters: The Disillusioned Generation.* Chicago: Northfield Publishing, 1994.

3. Langford, Jeremy. *God Moments: Why Faith Matters to a New Generation.* Maryknoll, NY: Orbis Books, 2001.

4. Beaudoin, Tom. *Virtual Faith: The Irreverent Spiritual Quest of Generation X.* San Francisco: Jossey-Bass Publishers, 1998.

5. Opperman, Scott. "Notes on Generation X for Charis Ministries." (unpublished)

6. See studies by Barna, noted before, and William V. D'Antonio, et al., in *American Catholics: Gender, Generation and Commitment,* Altamira Press, 2001; Dean R. Hoge, et al., in *Young Adult Catholics: Religion in the Culture of Choice,* University of Notre Dame Press, 2001; and James D. Davidson, et. al., in "NCR on American Catholics," *National Catholic Reporter Online.* September 30, 2005.

7. Langford, Jeremy. *God Moments.*

8. Reese, Mary Anne. "Refracting the Light." America 189 (8). September 22, 2003.

9. D'Antonio, William V.; Davidson, James D.; Hoge, Dean R.; Gautier, Mary L. *American Catholics Today: New Realities of Their Faith and Their Church*. Lanham, MD: Rowman and Littlefield, 2007.

10. Ibid.

11. Smith, Christian. *Soul Searching: The Religious and Spiritual Lives of American Teenagers*. Oxford, New York: Oxford University Press, 2005.

12. Reese, 189.

Chapter 2

1. Joyce, James. *Finnegan's Wake*. New York: Viking Press, 1939.

2. Buechner, Frederick. *Wishful Thinking*. San Francisco: HarperSanFrancisco, 1993.

Chapter 5

1. Hopkins, Gerald Manley. "God's Grandeur," in *Poems*. London: Humphrey Milford, 1918.

Chapter 8

1. Burghardt, Walter. "Without Contemplation the People Perish," *Church*, 1989.

Chapter 9

1. *Sons and Daughters of the Light*.

Index

A

advice-giving, 87–88

African Americans, 32–33

afternoon mini-retreats, 24

age diversity, 53

arts publications, advertising in, 26

audience

    appealing to diverse, 15

    connecting with, 70

B

balance in choosing team, 53–54

Barna, George, 9

Beaudoin, Tom, 9

bilingual events, 33

blaming, 87

Blessed Sacrament, 16, 38, 45, 103

body language, 71

breakout sessions, 24

Buechner, Frederick, 23

Builder Generation, 17

Burkhardt, Walter, 96

business cards, 27

business publications, advertising in, 26

BustedHalo.com, 27, 112

C

Called and Chosen: Renewing Our Catholic Commitment Retreat, 3, 121

Casas, Bartolomé de las, 20

Catholic Church

    institutional, 14

    young people and, 19, 20–23, 110–111

Catholic Network of Volunteer Service, 112

Catholic traditions
  linking life struggles to, 51–52
  weaving in elements of, 16–17

Charis, defined, 2, 78

Charis Ministries, founding of, 1

Charis Partner site, 112

Charis Retreat, 5
  adaptations of, 115–124
  after, 105–114
  afternoon mini-, 24
  approach of, 8
  assumptions of, 7–19
  characteristics of, 78
  communal prayer on, 78
  connecting after, 110–113
  cost of, 30
  differences from other retreats, 2–3
  dynamics of, 39–49
  ending, 106–07
  etiquette, 16, 79–80
  format of, 78
  goals of, 7–19, 66
  grounding and theology of hospitality, 73–74
  models, 3, 120–22
  movements of, 36–49
  overview of, 77–79
  reasons to come on, 77
  resources on, 5, 30
  schedule for, 38–39
  shortened forms of, 24
  silence as key element in, 79
  small groups on, 82–84
  structure of, 36–37
  support network for, 126

Charis Seasonal and Topical Days of Reflection, 122–24

Chicago, Charis retreats in, 39, 62, 77, 79, 81

Christ Renews His Parish, 2

chronological narrative, 70

Cincinnati, Charis program in, 24, 29–30, 32–34, 39, 62, 77, 79, 81, 111, 118

closing prayers, 99

communal prayer, 78, 99

community, forming, among team members, 57–64

concern, exploring issues of, 43

confidentiality, 38, 86–87

consumerism, 9

cross-talk rule, 88

cultural awareness, 9–10

Cursillo, 2

Cusick, Fr. John, 125

D

days of prayer, 24

deadlines, 31

Decisions! Decisions! and Transitions That Follow Retreat, 3, 122

dinner

Friday-night, 82

reunion/post-retreat-evaluation, 63–64

diversity

age, 53

ethnic, 31–34, 53

gender, 53

in personalities, 54

in professions, 54

racial, 31–34

in spiritualities, 54

in vocations, 54

divine reading, 102

Drexel, St. Katharine, 20

E

e-mail, 27–29, 56–57

ethical responsibilities, 46–47

ethnic diversity, 31–34, 53

etiquette, 16, 79–80

eucharistic adoration, 103

Eucharist, celebrating the, 49, 99–101

evaluation, 49, 107–10

evaluation/reunion meetings, 63–64

Evangelical Protestants, 10

evening gatherings, 24

examen, 16, 38, 42, 101

F

facilitation, small-group, 61–62

facility, 123

faith-sharing talks, 65–72

fast-forward, 70

feedback, 60–62, 68

final blessings, 101

focus groups, 29–30

follow-ups, 110–112

Friday-night meeting, 40–41, 63

Friday-night-to-Saturday-afternoon events, 24

G

gender diversity, 53

Generation X, 7, 11–12

Generation Y, 7, 11–12

goodbye, saying, 49

ground rules, establishing, 40–41

group norms, 86–88

group prayer, 58

growth, resources for, 17

guided-imagery prayer, 38, 102

H

healing, resources for, 17

healing prayer, 46, 98–99

Hinduism, 10

Hipskind, Tim, 32

homily, 48, 101–102

Hopkins, Gerard Manley, 65

house logistics, 80

house parties, 29

I

icebreaker, 81

ice-cream social, 47

Ignatian spirituality, 1–2, 12–13, 65

Ignatian contemplation, 38, 42

improvements, suggesting, 61

individual reflection, 37

innovative ritual and liturgy, 2

institutional church, 14

introductions, 58, 76

invitation, 73–74

Islam, 10

J

J.A.B.-ing (Judging, Advice-Giving, or Blaming), 38

Jesuits, 2

Jesus Retreat, "Who Do You Say I Am?", 118–20

Judaism, 10

Judeo-Christian tradition, 65

judging, 87

K

KAIROS teen retreats, 2

L

lay of the land, getting, 20–23

leaders, 21–23, 32, 111

lectio divina, 16, 102–3

life experiences in choosing team, 54–55

life struggles, linking, to Catholic traditions, 51–52

lights, 44–45

listening, 55, 97

liturgical music, 33

liturgy, 48–49

Liturgy of the Word, 98

logistics, 80, 123–124

Loyola, St. Ignatius of, 1–2, 13, 16, 42, 58, 65, 102, 104, 118, 125

M

Marriage Encounter, 2

married people, 54

Mass, 14, 38, 100

celebration of, 42, 49

mass marketing, 9

meditation, 45, 102

meetings

evaluation/reunion, 63–64

Friday-night, 40–41, 63

during retreat, 63

team, 57–60, 94

Mello, Anthony de, 93

Millennials, 7, 11–12

ministry of prepared peers, 13–14

Moralistic Therapeutic Deism, 12

morning prayer, 41

Mother Teresa of Calcutta, 20

movement prayer, 16, 38, 103

movements of Charis retreat, 36–49

multicultural ministry, 31–34

multigenerational conference, 24

multimedia, 14

music, 100

liturgical, 33

soft, 45

music video, 77

N

National Catholic Young Adult
Ministry Association, 113

New Age, 10

Nguyen, Peter, 118

No-J.A.B. Rule, 39, 87–88

O

one-on-one, praying, 96–97

opening prayer, 77

opening session, 76

openness, 15, 55

outdoor prayers, 96

overcommitments, avoiding, 56

P

participation, encouraging, 18

passing, 87

pastoral coordinators, 45

pastoral counselors, 17

pastoral ministers, 46, 58

Paulist Fathers' young adult
ministry, 27

Pause Rule, 85

Peace and Justice: Catholic Social
Teaching Retreat, 121

peers, 13–14

presentations by, 36

personal identity, developing, 8

personalities, diversity in, 54

pop culture, 14

praise, soliciting, 60–61

prayer(s), 39

closing, 99

communal, 78, 99

days of, 24

group, 58

guided imagery, 38, 102

healing, 46, 98–99

learning new ways of, 42–43

morning, 41

movement, 16, 39, 103

one-on-one, 96–97

opening, 77

opportunities for, 15

outdoor, 96

small-group leadership training, 62–63

Taizé, 103

prayerful reading of the Scriptures, 102–3

prayer service, 101–3

prayer support, 94

prepared peers, 13–14

pre-retreat hospitality, 74–75

professions, diversity of, 54

promotional methods, 25–34

purpose, need for clear, 69

R

racial diversity, 31–34

radio, 27

reconciliation, 97–99

reflection, 2, 40, 44, 78, 79, 81, 122–24

relationships, developing, 8, 18–19

religious language, 71

retreat overview, 77–79

reunion/post-retreat-evaluation dinner, 63–64

ritual, 44–45

rosary, 16, 42

S

sacrament of reconciliation, 39, 97, 98–99

sacred silence, 95–96

Scriptures, 100–101

prayerful reading of, 102–3

Second Vatican Council, 2, 7, 11, 14

Seekers' Retreat, 16, 39, 48, 115–18

Sex in the City of God: Faith, Intimacy and Relationships Retreat, 121

silent reflection, 2, 37

single people, 54

slices of life, 70

small groups, 15, 37–38. *See also* teams

depth of, 84–86

facilitation, 61–62

initial sessions, 89

life cycle of, 89–90

overview of, 82–84

prayer leadership training, 62–63

problems within, 90–91

sharing, 2

winding up sessions, 90

Society of Jesus, 2

soft music, 45

Spirit at Work Within: Discerning Our Gifts, 3, 121

spiritual concerns of young adults, 10–12

spiritual direction, 17, 39, 96–97, 113

Spiritual Exercises, 2, 13, 16, 58, 118, 125

spiritualities, diversity in, 54

spiritual resources, 93–104

stories

choosing, 68

linking with our faith tradition, 71–72

sharing, 65–72

tone of, 70

support, developing base of, 23–24

T

tai chi, 103

Taizé prayer, 103

talks, 36, 59–60, 65–72

building blocks for, 37

faith-sharing, 65–72

Friday night, 40–41

mentoring, 67

retreat, 37, 65–72

Saturday evening, 44–45

teams. *See also* small groups

diversity, 15, 53–54

evaluations of, 109–10

forming community among members, 57–64

introductions of, 58, 76

inviting members, 56–57

meetings of, 57–60, 94

selecting and preparing, 51–64

training, 58–60, 62

theme, need for clear, 69

time considerations, 86

timing, 31

tone of stories, 70, 71

traditional devotions, 103

training, 58–60, 62–63

V

Vatican II. *See* Second Vatican Council.

visual promotion, 26

vocations, diversity of, 54

vocations directors, 39

voice, tone of, 71

W

Web sites, 27

welcome, 73–74

"Who Do You Say I Am?" The Jesus Retreat, 118–20

work, developing definition of, 8

X

Xavier, St. Francis, 20

Y

young adults

    applying our knowledge of,
        13–19

    Catholic Church and, 19, 21–22,
        111

    needs of, 8, 10–13

    Paulist Fathers' ministry, 112–113

    spiritual concerns of, 10–12